The Ghost of Fountain Courts

Linda Gatewood

The Ghost of Fountain Courts

The Ghost of Fountain Courts

Published in the United States of America
ISBN: 9781096992318
Imprint: Independently published
1. Supernatural; Biography & Autobiography
2. Nonfiction/ General

Other books

by ***Linda Gatewood***

The Winter Secret Series

Winter Secret

Spring Promise

Summer Truth

Autumn Hush

A Chance to Remember

The Legend of Clevenger's Lost Gold
Co-authored with Aaron Werner

Soon to be released:

Timely Rendezvous

Acknowledgement

Most of all, I am grateful for my sister, Tyke, who went through most of this with me. Her memory of these events reinforced the story and added details not to be forgotten.

As usual, I owe a great debt to my favorite editor and dear friend, Jan Domenico. I appreciate her sharp eye and honest appraisal – a gal of many talents!

Thanks to my daughters, Jenny and Rachel, for their continued support, and to my son, Aaron Werner, author of *The Legend of Clevengers Lost Gold*, for his technical skills and advice.

Also, thanks to Vicki Miller (a long-time friend who understands) for her kindness in beta reading. I want to thank Lisa Melton, a talented writer, who generously read and approved this book and helped me in my decision to publish.

I dedicate this book to those who love a good ghost story – especially if it's true!

Preface

I did what all young girls did in 1964. I kept a diary; the old-fashioned kind with a lock and key. Every day, I faithfully poured out my heart, describing events and deeds that happened to me, along with the emotions that I felt. It would have been like any other teenagers diary, except for one thing – the carefully recorded details of a haunting! A true, yet terrifying ghost story, that occurred during the turbulent 1960's.

The events I described happened to me during that vulnerable and impressionable time. In my innocence, I wrote it all down.

I hid my diary away where it was lost for 30 years. It rested inside a box, put away and forgotten while life continued to happen. When I finally found it again, one spring-cleaning day– damaged and mildewed – I copied it. I threw away the damaged original, but kept my youthful scribbling. Even though the content was disturbing to me, I just couldn't let go. The copy was folded and tucked into an old filing cabinet where it was forgotten for another 20 years.

It has taken a long time before I had the courage to revisit the terrifying events.

Along with a record of the haunting is a difficult story of hidden secrets kept within a family for decades. Facing those dreaded events while confronting a terrifying haunting, collided in time, and brought me to a pivotal moment.

This is the story of that day. I will tell you the true story about my haunting.

Ages Ago…

When I was just fifteen, almost sixteen, in the mid-nineteen sixties, my dad bought an ugly, old place in Pocatello, Idaho with plans to renovate. Located on the edge of one of the oldest parts of town and in an adverse neighborhood, it nestled below the southern foothills. The city of Pocatello was bordered on two sides by generous hills and mountains before it touched against a valley that stretched to the edge of an ancient lava flow. Back up in the foothills, a creek flowed nearby and separated the lower foothills from the city section of the original old town. It seemed to be a dividing line that isolated the neighborhood from the once, bustling old part of town that now held more and more empty buildings.

Pocatello was a railroad town, an important hub of networked tracks and a traveler's interlude. During its heyday, it harbored and dispersed trains from every direction and managed distribution of a myriad of cargo. Mostly a blue-collar town, its vibrant, rich history melded people together in unbreakable bonds. Protecting its own, it gathered a sheltering arm around families and kept their secrets for generations.

One fateful day, we all piled into my dad's new 1963 Lincoln Continental to go look at the recently purchased house. At that time, I was optimistic. My folks described it as a large home with lots of room and a large courtyard in the back. Doesn't that sound fabulous? I envisioned a tennis court or large area for parties and entertainment.

With these thoughts I asked, "So if it's big, do I get my own room?"

"Of course."

That was all I needed to hear. I had always shared a room with my little sister while my older sister had her own. I was older now and wanted my own room. I'd become obsessed with having a spot all my own where no one was allowed to trespass.

My anticipation was high as expectations magnified and when we pulled up in front of our new home, I could only stare in shock.

The monstrosity my parents had just purchased covered half of an entire block on the street. It predated most of the current houses and consisted of a shambles of apartments to be rented out, some located on a second story, all squeezed together in a large "U" shape fashion. I'm sure my bottom jaw dropped while my mouth hung open. This was not at all what I expected. It didn't look like the house I'd envisioned.

Built in the early 1900's, the complex dominated the block. The front was a two-story high, white weatherworn clapboard building, with windows on both floors. At first glance, it resembled a large warehouse, plain and simple with no molding or décor on the outside separating the second floor. Its stark, shabby affront warned off a casual visitor. There was no welcoming entrance along the front, no path leading guests inside. Visitors were greeted by a blank wall with windows that stared back with hollow, vacant eyes.

Our front door was just around the corner where a walkway lined with scented lilac bushes led inside.

I followed my mom to the door and mumbled, "This place is a dump."

"Honey, you have to look at it with eyes that can see how beautiful it will be someday."

Squinting against the hot sun, I asked, "Where's the courtyard?"

"It's in back."

I followed as she led the way along the walkway that flowed around the side of the odd shaped building.

The "U" in the backside, had stairs that ran up to the second floor with a balcony on the inside leading to the separate apartment entryways. Standing in the courtyard was comparable to being center stage surrounded by bowl-shaped seating. Looking up, the empty window eyes watched.

Part of one side was only a one-story section and that was where we planned to live. It was large and roomy, promising comfort for our family.

Down in the courtyard there was a building located right in the center known as the bathhouse. It held an old-fashioned washing machine, a room with a big claw-foot bathtub, and evidence of a public restroom, now removed.

Like my mom suggested, I tried to imagine that once upon a time, the tenants would gather in the courtyard and visit. It must have been cozy, with people using the bathhouse for washing laundry on the old machines and hanging clothes on lines that were no longer there. The use of the claw-foot bathtub was a more curious consideration. Whispering to my mom, I asked, "Do we have to bathe out here?"

She laughed and answered, "I don't think anyone has done that in years."

When I first walked around the complex, it was obvious that everything had been neglected for a long time. It was ugly and I felt embarrassed that this would be my new home. Remembering my mother's encouraging words of *charming, quaint*, and *antique*, the only word that came to my mind was *dreadful*!

The outside stair railings leading up to the second floor were weathered and full of slivers just waiting for a careless hand. Weeds grew abundantly in all the cracks of the large concrete courtyard and caught in my sandals as I wandered around in my investigation. The windows above on the second floor stared at me, as if silent watchers still inhabited.

Mom encouraged, "Go ahead, climb upstairs and look around."

Rubbing my hands over my shorts, I said, "No thanks, it looks dangerous up there."

The heat of the sun beat down in the vast unshaded area and soon drove me back around to the side; this was where our apartment was located. The small yard was cool with large, old shade trees that still stood strong.

To get there I had to walk past the far back of the lot, behind the apartments, where two small houses stood that were also part of the purchase. They were separate and apart from the main building, and would be rented out.

Mom called, “Are you coming inside with me?”

“In a minute.”

Sitting in the shade of the trees, I contemplated my new home. I wasn’t happy about it and almost felt ashamed that I didn’t agree with mom about its potential. I had no enthusiasm for this move. Of course, I knew she was simply supporting my dad. He was the one who wanted this.

No one currently lived in the bigger apartment, and only a couple of the other apartments were rented. They were all pretty shabby. The complex was a good buy, since no one seemed interested in taking on such an enormous job. That was why my dad purchased it.

Most of the rooms had been boarded up and stored with junk for many years. My father planned to open them, install or repair the plumbing, add new paint, renovate and rent them out mainly to college students. It was a brilliant idea that could generate a good second income, since our city was a college town and housing units in great demand.

I stood up and brushed the grass from my legs. Glancing at the front door, I walked in that direction. When I stepped inside, I called, “Mom, where are you?”

“Over here,” she answered.

I followed her voice.

This new home was a novelty to us, as we were accustomed to having a bathtub in the house where we lived, not outside in a courtyard; the shower in our apartment would have to suffice.

Since we were moving into this ugly place, we planned to live in the side of the "U" that had no second floor and was the largest in the complex.

Our family apartment had three bedrooms and one bath. The small front yard was located on the side street and was filled with the big shade trees sided by a band of mature lilac bushes that bloomed heavenly scented flowers every spring. It wasn't a large space, just a lawn-covered separation from the sidewalk that ran down the side of the building. The larger yard in front was not used because it had no trees or bushes, just lawn, and no privacy. It was also missing a front door to welcome visitors.

When she saw me, Mom asked, "Well, what do you think?"

Like a typical teen, I raised my eyebrows, as if astonished and replied sarcastically, "Really?"

She patted my arm, 'It will be nice when it's done."

"Where's my bedroom?" I walked down the hall and counted the rooms. "There are only three bedrooms," one for mom and dad, one for my older sister, which left one to be shared with my little sister.

Mom said, "Well, I have an idea…"

***

The restoration was a massive amount of work, and my dad, being healthy and smart, was well suited. Because he had a day job, he renovated in the evening and on some weekends, always with my mom beside him, working just as hard.

There was one unique element of interest on the property. A large fountain built of river rock sat prominently on the corner in front, with a second twin fountain positioned several yards down the side, amidst the old shade trees. Located along what must have once been the main road, but was now a side street, the road lead to a dead-end at the creek. The fountains stood sentinel on the property. I suspected that once there might have been a crude bridge at the end of the road that crossed the creek and led into town.

A modern bridge several blocks away was now used to cross over, isolating this part of the neighborhood from swift and easy access to city center.

The fountains were big enough for us to sit on the edge, looking down into what must have once been a water trough but was now filled with dirt and weeds. In the center, the circular body of the fountain made of river rock climbed five or six feet high, where it must have once bubbled out on top and cascaded down the skirted sides into the furrow. Although they no longer flowed with water, these two beautiful fountains were the reason the place was called Fountain Courts.

It was originally built in the past as a beer brewery called The Fish Drug and Bottling Co. makers of Ye Olde Tavern Club Beverages. That would have been before 1915 and the confines of prohibition. As a brewery, a local beer was produced and successfully consumed before it was changed to a soft drink facility when prohibition became the law. In 1918, it was converted into apartments called the Fountain Courts, so named I'm sure, because of the two fountains in front.

I didn't care who had built the monstrosity or for what it was originally used. I only cared that I had my own bedroom and didn't have to share with one of my two sisters.

Teenagers sometimes have tunnel vision and I certainly had mine!

***

June 3, 1963

"Dear Diary,

...Today was the awfulest day of my life and the best day of my life! Awful, because I saw where we are moving to – an ugly old house – but the best because I'm going to get my own bedroom! When mom told me it was a big house, I pictured one of those beautiful homes up along the bench – something new and stylish – but it isn't. It's old and in bad shape. Mom promised it would be better after all the work was done to restore it. I just don't know. One thing I hope for, though, is to have my own room! Cheryl got her own room when she was my age, so I guess it must be my turn!

The problem is, my room is a little harder to find..."

***

Our one-story apartment was shaped like an L – the kitchen/dining and living room located on the short end of the L; the three bedrooms on the long end of the L. Tacked onto the end of the long L was a small, old apartment, number fifteen, that had been boarded up for years and stored with junk. A wall separated it from ours and it had its own outside entrance in the courtyard, the door locked tight by a padlock. My mother figured that if we cleaned out that apartment and made a doorway that would connect it to ours, then I would be able to have my own room.

Mom patted my arm comfortingly and said, “It will take a lot of hard work but after that you will have a lovely room!” She had a way of opening up dreams and making them happen.

I had faith in her that my room would be everything I ever wanted. “I can help. I’m so excited!” My dreams began to form and I had wonderful ideas.

The plan was in place, but it took a whole year before we could work on the project. Restoring the other apartments was a priority whereas creating a bedroom for me was near the bottom of the list. I shared a room with my sister and dreamed of the day when I’d have my own.

I had no idea that on that day, I would begin my intrusion into a realm that obviously and indelibly belonged to someone else; someone who had kept silent for over a century, his presence hidden away long ago.

Early days of summer 1964

"Sometimes, I wake in the night, gripped again by the terror of the memory of the haunting. I listen and am once more terrorized by the ghost".

Revised diary entries dated June-July through mid-August 1964.

A year had finally passed and my patience was running thin. I wondered when I'd get my own room! Unlike my mom's long-suffering ability to endure, I was anxious to move to my own space and unable to understand the delay.

Mom had the patience of a saint when it came to spoiling us girls. Working with dad wasn't always easy, but she persevered until he was ready to allow us to start on the project. The day had finally come when it was time to work on my bedroom, and I walked with her into the courtyard toward the padlocked door of apartment number fifteen.

She stood before the unlocked outside doorway that led into the closed-up rooms. My long-awaited-for room was in there somewhere. I was excited to be able to do this, and couldn't wait to get started. Mom was almost as excited as I was. She knew how long I'd waited for this day and couldn't resist having fun at my expense.

"Wait! This lock won't open! I think its sealed shut!" Her expression glowed with delight.

For a moment, my brow creased in concern before I saw the smile hovering around her lips. I cried, "Don't tease me!" before I laughed nervously.

She lifted the lock off the latch and the door opened into a small, cluttered kitchenette piled with boxes, an antique table and chairs, and a big old dresser. Looking beyond, we saw a gloomy dark interior that was just as cluttered with more storage.

Standing still and staring all around, my mom said, "It's so full of stuff! Look at all that furniture! It's piled to the roof." Not one to fear hard work, she grabbed the edge of the old dresser covered heavily in dust, "Help me move this."

"Okay," I pulled with youthful vigor toward the door.

We had to pull everything outside, to make a pathway through, which meant making several trips back and forth, finally going down a few steps to the yard. When we finally created a walkway from the diminutive kitchen into the small living room, we were met with several feet thick of stored items in all directions that piled clear to the ceiling.

I pointed to the wall covered in storage that butted up against the tiny room that separated number fifteen from our apartment, "We should start there." I was anxious to get into the room that would be mine. "There must be a doorway behind all that junk."

My mom was a tiny person who worked hard. She was so pretty and knew how to make things attractive – including herself! Whatever project my dad decided to begin, she was ready and willing to shoulder her share of the work and did it with a cheerful heart.

She said, "Okay, let's get started!"

While sorting through the assemblage we found some lovely antique items that included a beautifully preserved rainbow jukebox and several old iron bed sets along with dressers and chairs. To me, all that stuff just looked old, creepy and dirty. I was at that teenager age where anything not brand new, was too old – including people approaching the ancient age of thirty.

For the past year, we had been refurbishing, cleaning, and repairing the other apartments to rent. Much of the furniture that was stored in the many rooms of the various units was cleaned and later painted, before being moved back into vacant apartments that had been renovated and eventually rented out to tenants. Number fifteen was the last to be cleaned out.

When we stopped for a rest, mom reached over and pushed my long hair aside, away from covering each side of my face.

"Peach blossom, I wish you wouldn't cover your face with your hair. You have such pretty eyebrows and when your hair hangs over like that, no one can see them."

I shook my head and let the hair settle back against my cheeks, "Don't be silly, this is the style."

My mom called us girls by pet names; I was Peach blossom, my little sister was Piggum and my older sister was Meathead – spoken in a soft voice, with lots of love! My little sister had a second pet name that stuck with her all of her life – Tyke! She was always a tiny little person.

I peeked between the curtains of my hair and began to work harder to uncover the wall that separated us from the room. "There should be a door here somewhere."

Mom said, "It must be behind this huge wardrobe. I don't think we can move it. We'll have to wait for some help. This doesn't look like it's been moved in a long time."

In an unusual house like this with its checkered past and adaptable usage, the possible discoveries were numerous. The large Victorian dresser, heavily weighted and embossed, blocked our way to finding the door to my room.

We went back into the house to wash our hands. Mom glanced at the time, "Better get dinner started. Your dad will be home soon."

My dad expected dinner on the table when he came home from work. He was usually irritable and moody, so mom tried hard to please him. She was able to do this because she worked away from home at night, giving her the daytime to be a homemaker.

I needed to change my clothes and went into the bedroom that I shared with my little sister, Tyke. She was looking through a box in the closet. No one had a sunnier disposition than my little sister.

Her pretty, blond hair bounced around her face, "Found it!" she announced.

Tyke held up the red-haired troll while her blue eyes shown in happiness. We were close in age and could almost read each other's minds.

I asked, "Who are you trying to bribe, now?"

"I promised Laura that I'd give her my most treasured possession if she would pick up a snake and put it in the jar."

Trying not to laugh, I observed, "That troll sort of looks like Laura with all that red hair."

She laughed, too, "At least she doesn't act like one!"

"I know that troll is not your most treasured possession."

"She doesn't know that!" Tyke laughed and ran out of the room.

My sister was brave and wasn't afraid to touch a snake or a frog. She envisioned them as little people with tiny hearts. Making Laura pick up a snake was her way of helping a friend see the good in all things. Even though mom usually called her Piggum, I always called her Tyke. Mom played a game with her when she was little. "Whoever can say '*Piggum*' first is the winner." No matter how hard Tyke tried, she could never say it faster than Mom could. Years later, Mom admitted she only said "gum" – and that was how she always won!

That evening the TV was on during our family meal, broadcasting national news which was always disturbing. Since the assassination of President John F. Kennedy last fall, the country had been going through a troublesome time.

I chewed my food and listened as the broadcaster swiftly recounted the story. *"When the assassin, Lee Harvey Oswald, had been found, he'd quickly been assassinated, by Jack Ruby. In March of this year, Ruby was found guilty for killing Oswald."*

It seemed little comfort in the end for losing a great president, and America was unsettled. The continuing conflict in

Vietnam, the contradictory maneuvering and decision making by the government, created a great loss of confidence in our leaders. When it came to war, my dad, a WWII vet, had some strong opinions. He always blamed the politicians.

The mindset of my age group seemed to be that old people knew nothing and that was why we had these problems. The insecurity and unrest this outlook caused defined the decade of the turbulent 60's.

As a young person, it was natural to feel as if events were happening for the first time to only my generation. As my history teacher liked to say: *"History repeats itself as only human nature can and only wisdom can create the balance between the decades."* The mid-sixties not only had youthful innocence but also great industrial and technical strides that propelled us into an uncertain future.

I was blissfully unaware of what lay ahead but uncomfortable with present trends, as were most of my friends.

The TV had some good news as it followed the rebuilding of Alaska after the Good Friday earthquake, the most powerful earthquake so far in U.S. history (9.2). It happened in March, killing 125 people and inflicting massive damage to the city of Anchorage, Alaska.

I had finished my meal and was helping mom clear the table. She said, "Do you remember the earthquake in 1959?"

"Sort of."

"The Yellowstone Earthquake that devastated Hebgen Lake. We had been camping there but came home early. Remember?"

I answered, "I remember now, we got home late and I went to bed but the house shook so bad, it nearly threw me onto the floor!"

"Yes, it was strong, even this far away." We were over a hundred miles away on that night, but were still literally shaken from the destructive force of nature.

Dinner was finally over and we could get back to work. It took three strong men to move the heavy wardrobe aside and expose the hidden door. By the time we found it, the sun had set long ago. The door wouldn't budge; it was stuck solid and would require a good oiling in the hinges to loosen it. My dad took care of that and said it should sit overnight.

We went back to the house where my older sister, Cheryl was talking on the phone, keeping her voice low as she stretched the phone cord as far as possible from the surrounding noise.

Mom commented almost to herself, "I wonder why anyone would cover a door like that," thinking of the door to the hidden room. "Obviously, they couldn't use the room with that big old wardrobe blocking the entrance. Of course, I'm sure the door was blocked when the furniture was stored, but why close off the only way into the other room?"

I barely heard what she said, as I was so focused on listening to my older sister's conversation on the phone. Cheryl was so pretty and had many friends, especially since she worked at the newspaper.

That night when I went to bed, sharing a room with Tyke. I told her, "This will be one of the last nights I'll be in here."

She smiled, happy that I was happy.

"Dear Diary,

... Soon I'll be writing in this book while I'm in my new, very own room! I can't wait! Ever since we moved into this old place, I feel the need for privacy. Now that there are renters moving into some of the finished apartments, I need my own space. Things are changing more every day and I don't understand the unrest I feel. It's like reaching forward and believing in dreams that are only wishes. The unrest pulls me from my settled peace of mind and I need my own space to sort it all out..."

***

The next morning, I woke early and was looking forward to the moment when we would open the door. After mom was ready, we went out to the old apartment. The kitchen had been cleared out the day before and the living room had much of the storage removed. What remained was pushed to one side, including the huge dresser that now leaned against a different wall.

Between the two of us, we pushed on the door that had been hidden behind the old dresser. It opened to reveal a small room stored with a few pieces of furniture. The light was dim because the single window was concealed by years of dirt and debris. Standing in the middle of the room, I stared around at the walls. It had a feminine feel about it with a delicate, but dirty, rose petal patterned wallpaper on one wall. The hardwood floor was so dusty that our steps left footprints. Even though it was the middle of a very hot summer, I felt a cold draft brush my shoulders that caused goose bumps to rise on my arms. I took a step and my foot brushed against something lying on the floor. When I looked down, the dried carcass of a blackbird lay forgotten.

Mom said, “Hope that’s the only dead thing in here.”

To her surprise and delight, the items in there were at least fifty or more years old, having been closed up and locked away much longer than any other room in the entire apartment complex. We discovered an old treadle sewing machine and some lovely antiques that were draped in dust and cobwebs.

The space wasn’t stuffed with furniture – it just looked like someone shut the door on an ordinary room. The window was covered from both the inside and outside, so it was dark and felt as if it had not shared itself with anyone in many years. It was stuffy with dust and needed fresh air.

Mom handed me a pair of gloves. “Let’s get to work.”

After carrying out most of the items, I twirled around the newly cleared area and exclaimed, “This is great; my own room!”

“It’s so dirty in here that it needs a good scrubbing before you move in.”

Feeling grateful and happy, even the old ancient furniture made me optimistic. “Look at this antique dresser and matching bed! Can I use it? It’s so pretty.”

“With some cleaning, a new mattress and a coat of paint, I agree that it will look nice. We could cover the headboard with padded satin and quilt it with some pearls. Would you like that?”

That was my mom – always making ordinary things unique. She wanted it to be special for me.

We pushed out the larger items and added to what was left stored in the outer rooms, creating a pathway that led between the storage, through the living room and kitchen, to the back door and into the courtyard. In fact, for now, that would be the only way I could get to my room until my dad cut out the new door through the wall that would connect to the house.

Even though this old apartments’ outside door rattled the single windowpane whenever it was opened, my dad could fix it and maybe add a new door with a good lock that would keep me safe. I didn’t mind that I would have to run outside from the house and into the back courtyard in order to get to my room. I knew it was only temporary and, besides, I was just so happy to finally have my own bedroom!

With visions of a fairy princess room dancing in my head, I set to work, helping my mom do what needed to be done.

It started…

"My ears strained to hear the ghostly sound..."

It took several days before I could move in. Mom filled a bucket with hot sudsy water and began to scrub. After that, the colors on the walls were finally clean enough to see and the hardwood floors shone with a new light. It was decided that the walls looked good and didn't need new paint. The wallpaper on the single wall was cleaned and the delicate pattern was beautiful. The single window that had been covered over on the inside by storage, and on the outside by years of dirt and heavy foliage, was finally cleared and let in much needed light.

I painted my furniture while mom worked on the satin rose-colored and pearl-quilted headboard. Luckily, the dresser I'd found had rounded corners, glass knobs on the drawers and an old art deco styled beveled mirror. The pale pink paint that I used complimented the satin headboard and blended it all together.

When it was done, I stood in my doorway and looked at the bed all set up across the room. It was beautiful. I had the loveliest room anyone could ever want, and it was like a dream come true. For the first time in my life, I had a secluded place where I could put my stuff so that no one would snoop. Girls my age treasured privacy.

I loved to read and the first thing I did was organize a bookshelf with my favorite books. The small bedroom closet had originally been a bathroom but since it had long ago been disconnected, it was cleaned out for my closet and I filled it as full as I could with clothes and shoes.

I kept the door shut that separated my bedroom from the outer living room that was stored with miscellaneous items and led to the tiny kitchenette. None of the plumbing worked in the kitchen so it was just another storage room. The old door that led into the courtyard had a broken lock on it, so it was never locked. I used that way to go back and forth from my room into the house. There was a front door on the street side of the apartment in the old living room, but on the inside it was covered with storage, besides, it had been permanently sealed shut. No one ever used that door.

For the first time in many years, someone now lived in one of the rooms of number fifteen! The dust had been cleared and swept away in that bedroom, and fresh air filled the space. The sun now peeked through the window and glowed on the hardwood floors.

***

"Dear Diary,

...I'm finally settled in and everything is wonderful! All of my stuff is put away and I have plans to draw some great pictures to hang on the walls. I have visitors sometimes but mostly enjoy my privacy. One thing is strange, though. I feel a sense of there being no boundaries in here, as if the walls could disappear. My mind slips away into daydreams and seeks after something – what, I don't know. Something captures my soul and carries it away.

I listen for something –a sort of hush, a whisper that only consists of air that moves. The walls might vanish if I wanted them to; a timeless quality defines the space. It's hard to describe and sounds crazy - but it doesn't scare me..."

***

My family would sometimes come out to see me when I was in my room – to talk about something special – or just to visit. I loved having my own area to entertain and the first few days were exciting. Everyone in the family knew how I'd longed for privacy so they were good not to overstay their welcome. There was one member, though who avoided going out there at all.

One night after dinner, Tyke walked with me to my room. She stepped just inside the bedroom doorway but wouldn't come any further. I wanted to show her the new project I was working on. Trying my hand at embroidery, I needed her opinion.

"See? I don't know if this stitch looks like a leaf or not. I might not be cut out to do this kind of stuff." I could tell she wasn't listening to me. She was looking down at the floor. "What's wrong with you?" I asked.

"I don't like it in here. It just doesn't feel right."

"What are you talking about?"

Her eyes were big and her voice was almost a whisper. "I'm going back in the house." She turned and walked away.

Feeling hurt, I hollered after her. "Okay, see if I invite you out again!"

Miffed, I went back to my project.

Later that night, I was listening to music on the radio when the old back door opened. The loose windowpane rattled loudly, warning that someone was coming in. I heard soft footsteps before the bedroom door opened and my older sister, Cheryl, walked in.

Cheryl was the most beautiful girl I knew. She was a natural platinum blond who wore her hair in the popular pageboy style. When she smiled, it carried clear up into her eyes, as they sparkled with happiness. She wasn't expressively happy, it just bubbled inside reflecting her effervescence.

She looked around, examining the arrangement of the room and the lovely pearl quilted headboard. "That's so pretty. You're lucky." She smiled sweetly and stood beside my bed. "Aren't you lonely out here by yourself?"

"No." I hugged a pillow against my tummy while I watched her walk around and look at my stuff.

"Well, it feels a little creepy to me." She stared around at the shadows that climbed the walls, the little bed lamp giving off the only light.

Surprised, I answered, "Really? I don't feel that at all." I glanced out the window at the bright moonlight that peeked between the branches of the lilacs near the old fountain that stood in shadows. Nothing out there or inside my room scared me, because it was my own little place and belonged to me.

Cheryl came and sat beside me on the bed. Even though it was almost midnight, she wanted to tell me about her evening at the movies.

She was now living in one of the apartments with her new husband. She was still close to us and it was as if she was still a member of our immediate family.

Her eyes were shining as she talked about the actors in the movie.

When she stopped, I asked, "What else did you guys do tonight?"

"The usual – ice cream!" Her lip curled in a smile.

We talked for a bit and then she left, closing my bedroom door, her steps light before she shut the outer door, rattling the window.

I crawled into bed and turned off the light. I left my window open a few inches to let in the sweet smell of the lilacs from the bushes nearby. It was quiet and as I was dozing off, I heard loud voices coming from the other side of the wall, from my parents' bedroom. They were arguing again. Their fights had always terrified me because my dad had a violent temper.

I lay quietly, listening, hoping he wouldn't start to hit her again. My breath slowed while my heart pounded, the old fears engulfed me again, terrors from my childhood that seemed to be part of my blood and skin; memories long buried that came back, unbidden, but relentless. I listened until it was quiet and then I could sleep.

"Dear Diary,

... I'm so scared for my mom; scared for my sister, too. He's hurting mom again and it's awful. That old fear buried deep inside will never go away. I'm getting older now and can't wait to leave – but how can I leave my mom and sister behind with him, knowing what he does? I'm afraid to have friends over because he has secrets to keep and we aren't supposed to tell. I wish I could have girlfriends sleep over and play games all night. Mom said if he goes on one of his long-distance hunting trips, then maybe I can have a slumber party. That would be so much fun! Maybe for my birthday! ..."

***

My friends were not allowed to visit me in apartment number fifteen. Even though I thought it was unfair, I agreed because I wanted a room so badly. Sometimes, a friend who lived across the creek that separated our houses would come and visit outside my window. Steve wasn't my boyfriend, but I liked him a lot. One cool summer night, he came to visit. He stood outside the window near the lilacs while I stayed inside with the window open only inches, to talk.

"Hey, let me come in."

"No, I can't. I'll get in trouble if my parents find out."

He smiled while his blue eyes sparkled mischievously, "You don't have to be afraid. I wouldn't want you to get in trouble. They won't find out."

"I'm afraid they would."

"I'm only kidding," he teased.

Sometimes, when he teased me like this, I felt as if there were two meanings to his words. Right now, even though he spoke derisively, his voice soft and low, he was reassuring me that I could trust him – that he knew I was afraid of many things, but should never be afraid of him causing trouble.

He leaned against the window, his hand almost touching mine since I had placed it on the windowsill. "You need to come over and see the car my brother just got."

"That's neat. I thought your brother was going in the army?"

"He will if he has to."

I lowered my gaze, knowing the sensitive subject, “I bet you hope he won’t.”

He tossed back his head and chuckled, “I’m gonna go, when its time. I can’t wait to get out there and fight.”

Horrified, I objected, “Don’t say that. It scares me.” The subject of the Vietnam War that threatened to bring American involvement was an unsettling issue. Right now, we were on the doorstep of complete participation. All of my friends now faced the possible destiny of war, with fewer sympathizers every day. In fact, protesters against any association in the conflict were in the news daily. It was an unpopular war.

My dad must have overheard us from inside the house, because suddenly I heard the outside door rattle open and heavy steps march through the two outer rooms. I jumped away from the window before my door was shoved open.

He was angry and he charged in, yelling, “Who’s in here?”

Steve slipped away from the window, and I told my dad the truth – *no one was in my room*! I was shaking with fear, knowing how mean and unreasonable he could be.

He searched around the room, his eyes blazing with anger. He couldn’t look at me when he said, “Better not be anyone in here!”

He was a very handsome man and physically strong. Right now, his face was red and some of his hair hung loose across his forehead. His shirtsleeves were rolled up to his elbows and I noticed for the first time the gun he held in his hand.

This time he looked me in the eyes and said, “I’ll kill anyone I find in here. You remember that!”

After that, he left.

Tears stung and threatened to flow, because he scared me so much. I was also hurt because he didn't trust me. I wasn't a liar and I wouldn't break the rules.

I jumped when Steve whispered from the window, "Are you all right?"

Quickly wiping my eyes, I urged, "Go away! He'll find you!"

I could tell that he was shocked and angry – not at me, but at what had just happened.

He quickly looked away. When he glanced back, there was that smile again, lazy and arrogant. "That will never happen."

Then he was gone.

***

My dad intended to cut the door to connect my room to the house, but he was so busy working all day at his day job and remodeling the old Fountain Courts apartments in the evenings, that he never seemed to have the time.

I went to mom with my complaints. "It won't take very long. He just has to cut into the wall and make a door."

She looked away from me, her hands wringing together. "Yes, I know, it won't take much."

I added intensity to my plea. "When? He just keeps putting it off!"

She stood up and looked out the window. "Peach blossom, there's more to it than that. The opening will go directly into our room and there has to be a short hallway installed at the same time. You need your own door to be private – locked."

"So? That's not hard."

When she turned to look at me, I knew what she was saying. It was there in her eyes – the worry for my welfare – the motherly instinct to protect my sisters and me from him.

Ashamed of myself for pressuring her, I conceded, "Okay, I'll wait. Don't worry, I won't mind that much."

***

Weekends, when my dad wasn't working on the place, he would sometimes go boating or fishing. The summers were short in Idaho, and getting outside was important in the summer time.

Being an avid outdoorsman, Dad had a big boat and plenty of camping gear, so almost every weekend we would be either in Island Park, Palisades Reservoir, or out of state on a trip. On vacation, we would even go as far as Glacier National Park in Montana, stopping at secluded and beautiful lakes along the way to water ski and fish.

One of my favorites was Swan Lake up by Flathead Lake in Montana. With our bathing suits on, we'd jump into the icy water that was fed from melting snow on surrounding mountains. I thought about our trip last year, the first time we visited that lake. Cheryl still lived at home and we girls were swimming near the boat where it was anchored far from shore. My dad helped us into the boat to try a round of water skiing.

Mom didn't like boats so she stayed on shore and watched. She was just a tiny speck on the beach.

He grabbed his camera, "Okay, let's get a picture."

Feeling shy in my bathing suit, I grabbed a towel and covered myself, before scooting closer to my sisters, who were also covering up with a towel.

"No towels," dad ordered.

We shyly kicked them to the floor, our dread mounting at what was coming next.

"Now, don't sit so close to each other. Move apart, and Tyke, just bend over some but hold your head up."

She turned red and her brow lowered. Folding her arms across the bathing suit at her tummy, she tried to do as he ordered. None of us dared to question his orders. She was about 13 years old and starting to develop into a woman. Cheryl and I shared her discomfort.

"Now don't cross your legs; just open them apart."

The ordeal was soon over and we returned to skiing. The fun had gone out of the day and we were glad when it was done.

I blinked away the memories.

If my dad was too busy to cut the door, I didn't mind being separated from the house. I was just happy to have my own space to dream. There was a strange sort of relationship growing between that room and me. It was a safe harbor – an escape. Whatever you want to call it, I was feeling it. The atmosphere was both tempting and all engulfing. It was easy for me to spend hours and hours out there all by myself.

I could look out the small window and see the hedge of lilacs that bordered the yard. The fountain sat between the leafy bushes and my bedroom and was as large as its twin that was located further up in the yard, on the corner. It was right across from my window and I could see its' shadow when the moon was bright. Once upon a time, the rock object must have been considered a lovely creation. It was still imposing – tall and strong with layers of river rock that would have shown beautifully when water cascaded across the colored surface before settling into the trough. Right now, beautiful multi-colored petunias planted by Mom bloomed inside that area.

For someone who hated this place in the beginning, I was suddenly becoming very comfortable in my surroundings.

Sometimes on warm summer nights, my friends would come and get me and we'd walk to the nearby ballpark to watch a nighttime baseball game. Sitting on the bleachers in the balmy evening with cooling breezes wafting around us was heavenly.

Even though a few of the kids at school had started to dabble in the drug movement, popularized and promoted by music stars such as Bob Dylan and The Beatles – just to name a few who had embraced cannabis and promoted its use to the youth, I chose not to indulge. My folks didn't talk to us about drugs because it was not something that parents thought they had to worry about with their children. Many of my friends were religious and did what was right, but I also had friends who were tempted by the new popular pastime. Because it was secret and illegal, it was viewed as exciting by some kids and a way to escape from reality. Drug use was heavily promoted to my age group by those who profited, and we were an ignorant generation.

Luckily, I just didn't like the idea.

I felt as if life was being good to me – I had friends, places to go and best of all – my own beautiful bedroom!

"Dear Diary,

... Today, Janice picked me up to go get an ice cream. Of course, we went to our favorite place, mainly because she knew that Kenny would be there. She has such a big crush on him! I don't know about him – I saw him talking to Ed, who's known for selling LSD. Hard to believe a rich kid would sell drugs, but Ed does. He lives in a big house and his dad is an important businessman.

I wouldn't try that stuff for anything! It makes me mad when someone I know tries to persuade me. I just can't be friends with people like that!

The funniest thing, Tyke still won't come out to my room. She said it's too spooky. What a silly girl..."

***

When I'd been settled into my room for about two weeks, I was accustomed to the noises that were peculiar to the space, especially the old rattling outside door, whenever it opened and closed. The loose window sashayed in the frame and made a racket easily heard clear into my bedroom. If I was reading a book or writing a letter and heard that sound, I subconsciously knew that someone was coming out there. I was never afraid, because I felt safe, knowing only my family came out to see me. I usually kept the door closed between my bedroom and the rest of the empty apartment number fifteen.

One evening, when I heard the outside door rattle loudly as it opened and then slammed shut, I glanced at the clock, the hands at 11:00 o'clock sharp. I had stayed up late because I was deeply enthralled with a new book that I was reading, and assumed the visitor was my older sister, Cheryl. I went right back to reading, barely listening anymore. As my eyes scanned the words on the page, I faintly heard loud footsteps walk through the two storage rooms outside my closed bedroom door and I subconsciously assumed my sister was wearing boots or something.

The story that I was reading was *really good* and I hurried to finish the next few paragraphs before she came in. It was entitled *The Haunting of Hill House*. I usually didn't read that kind of book but it was on the list of good books to read. Surprisingly, I found it an enthralling story, well written and engaging. Since I didn't believe in ghosts, the story was more like a fantasy, but the characters were interesting.

It was a psychological thriller. As I read, the main character was sleeping inside the mansion, listening in the dark of night as the loud banging began hammering again against the wall, bouncing the pictures as they hung in their frames.

I lifted my head and paused…

It was a few seconds before I realized that my sister wasn't coming in. I didn't hear her leave, either, because the outside door hadn't rattled or the footsteps walk away.

For a moment, the quiet stillness that surrounded me suddenly washed over me, as I felt the tiny hairs rise slightly across my body. I stared at my closed door and for the first time, my breathing shook a little as I contemplated that someone else could easily have come in; some stranger – someone who wasn't a member of my family.

I waited for several minutes while I tried to rationalize what I'd heard. I imagined all kinds of scenarios – my favorite the one where Cheryl had come out, then changed her mind, tiptoed back and forgot to close the outside door when she left.

Scolding myself for being silly, I finally stood up and opened my door, calling out, "Cheryl, is that you?"

No one was there in the dark storage room. I knew I'd heard the rattling outside door open as someone entered and I heard the footsteps walk up to my door, but I heard no one leave. I walked all the way through the dark cluttered rooms and glanced around at the shadowed corners, until I faced the old outside door. It was closed. I opened it, the window jiggling noisily in the frame, and stepped outside. There was no one out there, no one on the path walking toward the back door of the house, no one hiding in the deep shadows.

The wind was blowing through the bushes while the single light that shown from the bathhouse roof lit the dusty courtyard revealing its emptiness. The trees swayed and caused the shadows to dance all around me.

Shivering, while goose bumps crawled up my arms, I went back into my room and wondered if I'd imagined it all. I glanced down at the book I'd been reading. Maybe the story had affected my common sense and I'd really just imagined the sounds. What else could it be?

I picked up the book and slowly closed it before tossing it onto the top shelf of my closet. I no longer wanted to read it.

The only other explanation was that my sister had come out to see me, changed her mind, and then left – and I simply didn't hear the door close. That sounded more logical.

It irritated me that she would frighten me like that so the next day I let her know that she'd scared me.

It was a warm sunny Saturday morning and mom had cooked a delicious meal for us. We were eating breakfast in the small dining room. Cheryl was there because her husband was at work.

Addressing my sister, I said, "You shouldn't come out without at least coming into my room!"

With a dazed look on her face, she asked, "What are you talking about?"

"You came out last night and left without coming in!"

Her mouth pulled into a frown, as she denied, “No, it wasn’t me.” She calmly buttered her toast and stared at me, her expression sincere.

I believed her.

Confused, I looked at Tyke. She said, “It wasn’t me! I’m not stupid enough to go out there in the dark. I was at Laura’s babysitting until her parents came home just before midnight.”

My mom said, “Don’t look at me. I was working and so was your dad. It was probably the wind. In an old house like this, there are many issues.”

My dad’s day job at the newspaper was a good paying job, but some evenings, especially on weekends, he sometimes joined my mom at work. She was an entertainer and played piano music in upscale dinner clubs. He was also a musician and sometimes played his clarinet in the same band.

I contemplated the exact events of the night before and couldn’t understand any of it. I finally decided that I must have *thought* I heard someone and been mistaken. Being so enthralled in that book, my imagination must have taken over when I heard some *other* noise that reminded me of the door opening and footsteps! Yes, that was it – or the wind.

For the rest of the day, feeling a little on edge and remembering the incident, I mostly stayed in the house, going out to my room for only a short time to clean. Back in the house, I watched TV until it was time to go to bed.

I walked outside alone, the stars bright above and the breeze soft under the tree canopy. The single light lit the interior of the courtyard, and it was vacant as I ran to the door with the rattling window. Hurrying through the dark kitchen and living room lined with boxes, I quickly shut my bedroom door, locking a hook latch that I'd added earlier that day. It wasn't strong enough to hold up to brute force, but it was at least some comfort to me. I peeked out the window at the great shadow of the old fountain as the dim light cast grooves into its rocky side. All was quiet.

Soon, I climbed into bed and closed my eyes, leaving on the radio as company against the sound of limbs scratching against the side of the building when the wind picked up. Minutes later, my groggy eyes closed, and I reached to turn off the radio before I fell asleep.

Suddenly, I woke in the middle of the night, the clock reflecting 11:00 sharp. The moon had disappeared and its gentle light was gone. Blinded by the dark, my heart beat faster. What had snapped me awake so fast? Then I heard the outside door open noisily, the window rattling loudly before it was slammed shut. Heavy footsteps moved through the outer rooms, right up to my bedroom door. Then silence.

I waited, wondering who it was, and was terrified as my heart raced, my breath suspended. Who would come out from the house at this hour? Was it Cheryl? If so, why didn't she open the door? Then I remembered the latch lock and was suddenly grateful to have installed it. If it was Cheryl, she would call out my name to let her in, but no one called out; no one knocked; no one twisted the knob to open the door.

When I tried to open my mouth to ask, "Who's out there?" my throat was dry and no sound came out. I was remembering last night and the same experience – which I *now knew* was not my imagination. After all, it was happening again…

I waited and listened while the wind outside picked up and moved the bushes to scrape at the window. I waited, listening for the footsteps to retreat – for the rattling window in the door as it opened– for the slamming of the door when the intruder left. I stared at the door wondering if it would crash open, kicked in by whoever stood on the other side. I waited while terror built inside of me.

As the long minutes crawled by, I knew I should get up and throw open the door – demand to know who was playing such a cruel trick on me! But I couldn't move. I was so scared that I just held still and wished to be invisible. I prayed it would go away.

Trying to find the courage to do something, I listened to every noise – the tiny scrape of a beetle that crawled across the floor; the flutter of a fly caught in the curtains, buzzing loud with annoyance.

As the moon reappeared through an opening in the clouds, the gray walls surrounding me were covered with shadows. Closing my eyes, I realized that I was hardly breathing, afraid that whoever was on the other side of the door might hear me and know that I was here. They must be out there because no one left. I didn't hear the footsteps walk away – didn't hear the window rattle or the door slam.

Presence

"The terrifying sounds are imbedded in my mind..."

The bright morning sun dappled through my tiny window and lay across the bed. I opened my eyes, feeling confused for a moment. Then I remembered. Somehow, I'd fallen asleep after waiting for a revelation that never came. I chided myself for being such a coward and not opening the bedroom door to confront the trickster.

With daylight shining everywhere, I felt more empowered, and after dressing, opened the door. Everything looked the same. Slowly, I walked to the back door. It was shut tight.

Going into the house, I told my family what had happened. Mom said I had a big imagination. My sister, Tyke, kept saying, "I told you it was creepy out there," as if it was the fault of my room. My dad had already gone to work, so I didn't have to hear his ridicule or anger – whichever he might have felt.

I was alone in my dilemma and questioned my sanity. They thought I'd imagined everything. Did I?

The day passed quickly, summer warmth and soft breezes making the time heavenly. Being a teenager in the summer was carefree, even though I always felt entangled in chores, conflicts and sometimes boredom.

The general mood of my generation was worried right now. Ever since the Vietnam War gained importance in our country, our plans for the future were somewhat muddled.

We were also mired in the new awakening of the injustice of racial discrimination. Just this last April, Mrs. Malcolm Peabody, age 72 (and mother of Massachusetts Governor Endicott Peabody) was jailed for 2 days in Florida for participating in an anti-segregation demonstration there. Just a month ago, President Lyndon Johnson signed the Civil Rights Act of 1964, abolishing racial segregation in the United States. This was promised as the turning point and absolute end of any former racial prejudice – at least that is what we hope.

I usually tried to tune out the tensions of my era by focusing on other activities. I enjoyed drawing and spent time practicing sketches of still life. I also loved to sew and usually had a project to work on.

Sometimes, on a warm weekend evening, I would "cruise" with my friends around the old Red Barn drive-in, then through town and back around again. All the boys at school were in love with cars, and showing off the amazing bodywork of a restored 1948 Ford Super Deluxe or a 1955 Blue Thunderbird in perfect condition represented the purpose of the cruise. It was a very *sixties* thing to do.

***

When evening came again, I was a little nervous. Convincing myself that someone had played a trick on me, I felt I needed to find out who it was. As comfort, I assured myself that it would probably never happen again and should stop worrying.

Going out to my room, I followed my usual routine, writing in my diary before opening the window to smell the fresh air. Flowers were blooming everywhere, and the scent was wonderful. Listening to the night birds was soothing. A car drove by, and nearby someone laughed loudly. This was just an ordinary summer night.

In spite of all my self-lecturing, I lay in bed, wide-awake, and listened to all the sounds an old house makes. I promised myself if I heard the footsteps again, I would simply open the door and catch the culprit. I was a brave person and could do that! Since no one else was going to take me serious and stop it from happening, then it was up to me, although, I was sure it would never happen again.

Dozing for a bit, I woke up – alert – and glanced at the clock. It was 11:00 o'clock. Then I heard the outside door open noisily, the windowpane rattled loudly when it slammed shut. Heavy footsteps stomped through the two outer rooms and stopped at my closed, latched bedroom door. Then, complete silence. I was frozen again, unable to get up and open the door. Fear coursed through my body while I argued with my cowardly self. Did I imagine those sounds as my family said I did? It was more than sounds; the heavy steps caused a vibration that I could feel as it seeped through the floorboards, across the floor and up into my bed.

I lay there terrified for a full ten minutes when suddenly I heard the outer door open, the windowpane rattle and light footsteps come to my door. Cheryl knocked quietly and whispered, "Are you awake? Let me in."

My eyes as round as saucers, I leapt out of bed and threw open the door. “Did you see him? He’s in here!”

“Who?”

“The footsteps…he never left!” Glancing around the dark storage room where all the shadows were hidden, I grabbed her and pulled her inside, closing the door firmly.

My hands clasped her arms tightly while I told her once again about the intruder who returned at night. This time she listened intently, without laughing at me. She said, “I think it’s creepy out here! I don’t know how you can stay here.”

I shivered and asked, “Can you stay with me?”

“Tonight?”

“Yes!”

“I can’t tonight because I need to sleep in order to go to work tomorrow.”

She saw that I was almost in tears, because she offered, “I can stay tomorrow night if you want. I think my great hubby will understand.”

“Will you?” Relieved that she would stay, I hugged her tightly.

She laughed, “Don’t worry, we’ll figure this out. Haven’t we always watched out for each other?”

Grateful for a big sister, I asked, “Why did you come out tonight?”

“I just wanted to talk. By the way, it’s funny that you wanted to have your own room so that you didn’t have to share with anyone, and now you are begging me to stay.” She chuckled to herself.

I considered her remark before answering, "Facing the boogieman with others is a lot better than confronting him all alone. This is the first time I've been alone at night."

"Is that all this is about?"

Regretting my words, I stammered, "I wish! No, this is really happening and it scares me!"

"You can always move back into the house. My old room will be empty as soon as I finish getting my things out."

"Mom put her sewing stuff in there and moved a piano in to practice on. The bed is gone. There's a small couch in there now."

Cheryl said, "I didn't know that. It's like mom's room now. She would love that."

After a silent pause, she told me about her day and shared all her news about her job. I loved to listen to her, and gradually my fears began to recede. It was comforting to think of normal things happening, even if it was just for a few minutes.

After she left, I was alone again and the anxiety returned. Exhausted and confused, I wondered if I really could be imagining this – dreaming it – or was it real? If it was real, why would someone want to terrorize me like this? Who would do that?

Finally, I fell into a troubled sleep.

***

The next day, I was happy all day and in a good mood because my sister was going to stay with me. Yes, it was ironic that I had wanted my own room so that I *wouldn't* have to share with a sister, and now I was ecstatic that one would stay with me for the night!

I cleaned and put fresh bedding on the bed. The sun was shining hot all day and in the daylight, it seemed ludicrous that when the night came, it might all change. Surely, the events would never happen again, especially now that someone else was staying with me, even if it was just for one night.

Watching the late afternoon news didn't dampen my hopeful outlook. The gloomy report that 5,000 more military advisers were being sent to Vietnam, bringing the total number of United States forces in Vietnam to 21,000, portended an ominous future. It was predicted that number could grow to over 180,000! I couldn't help but think of my friends – ready to graduate from High School in the spring of 1965 and prime to be drafted into the military.

When Cheryl came home from work, she stopped in before going up to her apartment. I reminded her about staying with me.

She answered, "Yes, I'm planning on it, but we are going out for a bit. I should be home by ten. Is that okay?"

Hiding my apprehension, my response was hesitant, "Yes, but please don't be too late!" I stared at the TV as a new show was starting.

My mom came in and turned off the TV. "Almost time for bed. Your dad went fishing with your uncle Jim. He won't be home till late tomorrow." She seemed to be relieved and was suddenly happy to have fun with us. In this mood, she was so funny to be around and made us laugh until our sides hurt.

That night, I waited for my sister to come home. Sitting comfortably in my room to read for a while, the night descended quietly. Checking the bedroom door, I discovered that the lock I'd added just the other day was broken. It dangled there, the screws pulled from the wood. Attempting to screw them back in, it seemed that the wood was gouged out and the screws wouldn't stay in place. I couldn't understand how the lock had been damaged and wondered if a family member had accidently torn it out. I'd been in my room or nearby for most of the day and hadn't seen anyone.

Pushing the unlocked door closed, I turned on the radio looking for good music, but found nothing. After endeavoring to read a book, but unable to concentrate, I laid it aside and thought about Cheryl, my beautiful sister. She was my half-sister to be accurate. I just never thought of her that way. She was just a toddler when dad married mom and a year later, I was born.

I felt protective of her, something we'd been taught all our lives. Whenever mom was away, we could never leave Cheryl alone, especially if dad was home. I was glad that she was married now and living away from him.

The clock ticked past 10 and I was getting nervous when the outer door opened, the windowpane rattled when it shut, and quiet steps approached my door – then it opened and there stood Cheryl! I was so happy to see her. She was in good spirits and talked about her evening while we got ready for bed.

"I saw Don on my way over here." Don was her old boyfriend, a student at Idaho State University who lived in one of our apartments. The subject of Don was a bit touchy. They broke-up just before Cheryl married her new husband. She was still confused about her feelings. She sat on the bed and curled her legs under her.

I commented, “I thought he was cute.”

“Of course, he was!” Her smile began to dissolve when she added, “Mom thought he was too old for me.”

We always listened to what mom thought because in our opinion, she was always right.

She asked, “Don saw me come in here. Do you think he’ll try to talk to me – tonight?”

“No, you’re married now. Mom said he wasn’t good for you, anyway.” I changed the subject. “Did you guys get a new car?”

“Oh, yes! It’s so nice!”

After a while, we turned off the lights and lay quietly.

I glanced at the clock, and it was almost 11:00 o’clock. My sister insisted on leaving the bedroom door slightly open to let in cool air after such a hot day. I was feeling secure and almost euphorically safe with her beside me. For some reason, I was positive that no one would bother me with her in the room. Besides that, it was most likely that everything that had happened before was simply my imagination! With her there, I wouldn’t imagine such frightening things.

We shared my full size bed and I closed my eyes, tired from a long day. The summer heat was getting hotter, and feeling the cool breeze that came from the open window and the slightly ajar door was soothing. I let myself relax and began to drowse. My nerves had been in a terrible state lately, and I was ready to believe that it was possible to have just imagined the sounds and disturbances. The start of school was not too far away, and this would be my last year in High School. It was unsettling to think about because there would be many changes ahead. I thought I was ready to leap into the future, but then again, I wanted to cling to the past.

Suddenly, I was brought abruptly back to the present. We both heard the outside door open noisily as the windowpane rattled loudly before the door was slammed shut. I glanced at my sister and her eyes were closed as if she slept, but I knew she was awake. The loud steps walked through both rooms and stopped at my door. Tightly closing my eyes, I waited. The door was open a few inches and nothing could keep the intruder from walking in.

Several seconds passed before my sister quickly sat up, jerking her legs against her chest. I sat up too and whispered, “Did you hear that? You heard him, didn’t you! It’s not my imagination!”

She stared around the room, her eyes bright in the darkness, “Yes! I thought it might be Don coming to see me. I heard the door slam, I heard the steps and I waited. Then I felt someone grab my feet! I thought it was Don, but there’s no one there!”

We both stared at the bedroom door, now wide open. She continued, “It wasn’t him! Someone grabbed my feet! I looked to see if Don…!”

She jumped up and picked up her clothes. “I can’t stay out here. This place is creepy! I don’t know how you can stay here. Let’s go inside.”

I huddled in my bed, “Don’t go!”

She ran out, slamming the outside door. I stared through the open bedroom door into the dark room that was piled high with storage, then slid out of bed and closed the door. I was shaking but was also angry that Cheryl had left. At least she had heard it – felt something – she knew it was true, and now, I knew it was true; I wasn't imagining this.

I had a witness.

I curled into my bed and wondered why someone would come to my room and grab my sister's feet! Who would do something so mean? Wasn't it enough to slam the door and stomp across the floor every night and frighten me? Did someone want to scare me away from my room? Who would want to do that?

I loved my room and no one was going to chase me out of it. Somehow, I had to find out who was doing this. This was *my room*! *Mine*!

Fright

Revised diary entries dated Mid-August – October 1964

Being cautious of whom I told about my quandary, there were a couple of friends that I trusted. You can always count on your friends to understand and believe in you. At least my friends believed me even if my family didn't consider my tale the truth. Since summer was in full bloom, my friends and I had lots of time to make plans.

The nightly visits – at exactly 11:00 every night, had become a dreaded challenge to me. I was so scared – watching the clock – sometimes staying in the house until well past 11:00 before going out to my room. It became a terrifying walk to make, not knowing who might be out there. The courtyard was dimly lit by a single light attached to a tall pole above the bathhouse, leaving many shadowy spots for hiding.

I never, ever ran into anyone, but always worried that I could. After all, someone was doing this to me, and I was afraid of whoever that was. They must be deranged or mad, a real lunatic to dedicate themselves to a nightly terrorizing of little ol' me.

My parents flat-out refused to believe me. Cheryl declined to tell them her story, afraid she would get in trouble for revealing that she was halfway expecting Don to come visit her out there.

She was also afraid that her revelation would get Don in trouble and possibly kicked out of his apartment. She was three years older than I was and so much more mature; but as long as she lived close by, she was still married to someone else.

My dad said that if I didn't stop talking about such nonsense, then I'd better move back into the house. He added that if it wasn't nonsense and some kid was doing that, then I'd better move back into the house. That was something I didn't want to do. By this time, I wanted my beautiful room right where it was. I decided to share my woes with only a few chosen friends.

After the incident happened when my sister was with me, her ex-boyfriend Don was keeping an eye out around the courts whenever he was there. He had listened to us tell our story, and being a macho super-hero, he kept a look-out whenever he wasn't in school or at work (which left very little time for him to be in his apartment).

My dad never, ever came out to my room because he was a busy person. Also, at that time, my parents were fighting more than ever. Dad was abusive and always had been. I was frightened for my mom and never forgot the many bruises she had sustained over the years as I was growing up. I was older now, and bolder, and had started to stand up to him when he threatened her.

She didn't like me to do that.

***

The summer seemed to be moving fast. There was always tension in our home, especially now. I think that clinging to the notion of having my room was a way of distancing me from our family problems. My 17th birthday had just passed by and I was almost a senior in high school. I wanted to hope for a better future.

Thank heavens it was still summer, albeit at the end of it, but I had some time on my hands. I sometimes worked as a babysitter for hire but that was usually a weekend affair. My attempt to find a full time job was unsuccessful. Sometimes I helped my mom work on projects for the Fountain Courts that kept me busy. Yes – I wanted to be independent and break away, but my mom and sisters needed me.

There were friends to hang out with and visits from aunts, uncles and cousins to endure. When I wasn't thinking of other things, I would focus on my problem with the nightly visit.

I have to confess that the most frustrating part of all this was my complete cowardice and inability to simply open my door when the offender stood on the other side. At the appointed hour, after the outside door rattled open and then slammed shut, and the heavy footsteps stomped loudly before stopping outside the door, all I could do was shiver in terror. I was a complete blathering idiot. That was when my imagination really took over and sent me into a world of fear like none other I'd ever experienced.

I stopped telling my folks about what was happening to me. Wanting to keep my room, I would do whatever was needed, so a plan was hatched, a way to catch the culprit and put an end to it all!

First, I systematically began to eliminate possible suspects and made sure I knew where everyone in my family was as each episode occurred. It required checking on each one before the appointed hour and then afterwards, to make sure they were still in the same place.

My little sister checked out and so did Cheryl and her husband; also, Don; that was easy. Next, my dad, who easily passed the test. He was usually working late or pounding away on a building project in his workshop at the Fountain Courts, or asleep. My mom also passed.

Each of my close friends were checked and rechecked, all eventually ruled out. Some of those were ruled out in bundles since many hung out in groups together at the same time. Next were casual acquaintances. They were soon all ruled out. I tested all of my friends until they were crossed off the list, one by one.

Next on the list were the closest neighbors and the few tenants. These I had to spy on to know their movements, and they were soon rejected as wrongdoers.

Even though I had to undergo the nightly visits as I checked off my list, I occasionally avoided that eerie routine by staying away until after 11 o'clock. It gave me a break from the tension. Finally, there were no names left.

You would think that the fear would go away after the ritual kept happening, but it didn't. Each time I had to endure the event, it was as terrifying as the first time. It was as if I felt the threat – the possible harm – from an unknown entity, whose menace was ominous and perilous. He could be a real person, a tangible threat, or worse, he could be inside my head. *No* – I wasn't imagining this!

I was desperate for help.

While I was muddling over the list, my mom came into my room. "Here's some clean clothes for you to hang up in your closet."

"Thanks."

"What are you doing?"

Reluctant and hesitant to share my crazy idea with her, I mumbled, "Sometimes I wonder about someone coming into my room."

She sat on the bed, "I agree. Do you remember a few years ago when that girl was murdered? I think she went to your high school."

"You mean, Vicki Jo Quinn?"

"Yes, it took a while before they found who killed her. I never told you that one of her murderers lived here." She reached out and pushed the hair from my face. "He was arrested and is now in jail. We thought he was a nice guy when he rented. Luckily, he was only here a few weeks before…I didn't want to scare you girls."

"That's scary." I thought about my efforts to spy on the tenants. "What apartment?"

"Number 6. We don't rent to people like that anymore. Your dad checks referrals carefully now. Come in the house; it's almost dinner time."

Nervous about what lay ahead, I followed her inside and watched TV. Once again, the news was unsettling as I listened to a long discussion about the publishing of the Warren Commissions Report, an official investigation of the assassination of United States President, John F. Kennedy last fall. Citizens still wanted answers about his death.

Later, in my room, I prepared for bed, glancing at the clock to check the time. It was only minutes away from the *eleventh hour*.

This time, I promised myself I'd open the door. All day, my courage was shored up, and I convinced myself that I could do it – *I could open the door!* I wasn't a coward and this time, I would prove it! I'd faced many fearful things in my life so far and could do this too!

My eyes were glued to the clock as the hands slowly shifted until it shown 11:00. Almost frozen as stiff as a marble statue, I stood by the bed when the outer door opened noisily. As the steps stomped across the floor, I too, took steps to stand in front of the closed door. When I knew he was on the other side, I believed my heart was thumping so loudly, that surely he could hear it. I felt a slight breeze brush across my legs from the open window, as sinuous as specter hands that try to catch hold.

I was terrified at what I'd see as I reached for the doorknob. My body was numb with fear, but I took a deep breath. For a moment, I thought I would pass out when the world seemed to tilt a bit as if an earthquake had thundered beneath my feet. Fear was surging through my veins.

My hand was stiff when I grabbed the doorframe and exhaled a shaky breath while I steadied myself. Placing my ear against the door, I listened for any noise of life on the other side. Stilling my own breath, I could only hear blood rushing through my body. It was silent on the other side.

The door was unlatched since the lock was broken, but I forced myself to proceed and placed my shaking hand on the knob, gripping tightly. My hand was slick with sweat. I stood there for several seconds listening to the great silence before I could bring myself to wrench open the door.

I had found the courage to face the intruder – I had opened the door! My eyes bulged as I tried to call out – *who's there? Who are you?* But my voice was gone as I stared blindly into the dark room. Nothing moved, not even me, as I stood there, exposed and ready to meet my tormentor. My skin was literally on fire, waiting for someone or something to grab me.

No one was there. My body was shaking too much for me to take a step, so I stood and waited. I gulped air as I glanced around the empty, dark room – the boxes stacked high, the furniture pushed against the storage boxes. I searched all the black shadows and strained my eyes to see behind larger items. I could see no shadowy figure or hear any threatening sounds. My first steps were hesitant as I continued to walk through until I faced the closed outside door, the one that had opened so noisily and slammed so loudly.

Behind me, the rooms seemed to vibrate with malice and shivers ran up and down my spine. Suddenly so scared I was afraid I'd lose my wits, I ran outside and raced into our house.

That night I slept in Cheryl's old room on the tiny couch surrounded by mom's favorite things.

***

The next morning I was perplexed at what was happening to me. Surely, there was someone doing this. I wasn't imagining it. Whoever had been there last night had disappeared without a sound. He'd vanished. How he could do that was a mystery.

It was urgent to find out who was doing this. Since I'd eliminated the people on my list, it had to be a stranger. To catch a stranger would take a new tactic.

At last, I had a plan. With the help of two of my most trusted friends (Steve and a friend who had previously been eliminated as a suspect), we decided that they would bring sleeping bags and sleep out by the back door. It was a rare opportunity since both boys had jobs moving pipes for a local farmer, an exhausting job that always required a good nights' sleep. Since they had to be to work at the crack of dawn, they were sacrificing their rest.

It was close to 10:30 when they arrived. I whispered, "Thanks for coming."

Steve grinned and nudged his buddy, "You can count on us."

Disconcerted by his facetious gesture, I was dead serious when I said, "Look, this is serious. Okay?"

Since my parents would never allow them to stay outside by the old back door, we had to sneak and do this. My dad was gone this evening and not expected home until late. The boys planned to push their sleeping bags under the small porch of back steps to hide. That way, they would be able to clearly see who was coming and going, but they would be hidden if anyone should come out from my house for some reason. If the unwanted intruder walked up the steps, they were strong boys and could wrestle anyone to the ground.

Boys are goofy and after the usual hassling from them, I said, "It's almost time."

I went into my room as usual and awaited the dreaded hour. It was dark and the boys were quietly hiding under the porch outside by the back door. They knew they had to be still because we didn't want to alert the intruder to their presence.

I was nervous and anxious as the clock moved closer and closer to 11:00 o'clock. That seemed to be the magic hour, the appointed time to torment me. I wondered who would be discovered in the scuffle after the boys grabbed the trespasser. Would it be someone I knew? Maybe the person would not come because they knew a trap was set. It was impossible to guess what would happen.

The clock finally ticked on until the hour came. I listened carefully. Suddenly I heard the outside door open and close noisily, the window rattling loudly, and then the footsteps thundered through the two outer rooms before stopping outside my bedroom door.

I listened for a ruckus as the intruder was caught, but all was quiet. In my mind, I was screaming, "Hey! Where are you guys? Don't you see him? Don't you hear him? Why haven't you followed him? Did you guys leave me alone?" The silence continued.

Time marched on, and I was too scared to move. I just stared at the door, now closed and unlocked because of the broken latch. It was so quiet. How could I open my door to go out? I was trapped here just as I always was. After time passed, I finally accepted the fact that the boys had abandoned me and left me here alone, or else they had played a trick on me.

The thought made me mad and I jumped up, threw open the door to an empty space, rushed through to the outside where I called out, “Where are you guys?”

“We’re here.” They crawled out from their bags from under the porch.

“Didn’t you see him?” I almost yelled.

Steve answered, “We didn’t see anything.”

“You must have heard the door slam!”

“We heard nothing. Honestly, we’ve been watching and waiting. You said 11:00 and nothing happened so we’ve just been waiting in case they were late.”

In disbelief, I asked, “Are you sure you were here? Did you guys leave for a bit?”

They could see that I was upset and rushed to reassure me, “We’ve been here. No one went in that door.”

I sat down on the step as the cool air wrapped around me. For the first time, I had to let go of all my doubts. I didn’t want to accept the fact that a ghost haunted me. That was a terrifying thought. I didn’t believe in ghosts. My parents didn’t believe in ghosts.

Suspiciously, I asked, “Are you sure you guys aren’t trying to scare me?”

Steve said, “Listen, we wouldn’t do that. If it helps, we’ll stay all night to make sure. Okay?”

I knew I could trust them. Steve was a special friend and knew about some of my family problems. He was sympathetic. We talked for another half hour before they left. They were both as dumfounded as I was and sincerely concerned about me.

They were my friends.

***

"Dear Diary,

...a terrible thing has happened. The noises – the footsteps – they don't belong to anyone. At least, not someone anyone can see. I think there is a ghost..."

Ghosts

"My stomach twisted again as I felt him near..."

In those days, no one believed in ghosts and if you did, you were considered a crazy person. Ghosts weren't logical and science couldn't prove they existed. Therefore, there was no such thing as ghosts. I had been taught as a child that I had a guardian angel who watched over me, and I always believed that an angel would guide me if I needed it. A ghost was different.

I had never seen a picture of a ghost because back then, there weren't many actual photos around. I was singular in my situation – there was no one to compare experiences. There were no ghost hunters on TV or special equipment for proving ghosts existed. In fact, there were very few who even believed they were real.

This wasn't something I dreamed up or invented. In fact, it was ruining my life; interfering with my hopes and plans – invading my thoughts – consuming my energy! I only wanted it to stop and yet, the courage to come face-to-face with an apparition eluded me. I accepted that I was being haunted. It was a very personal revelation to admit this to myself. I certainly couldn't tell my parents or my friends. Being provoked by a living breathing human being was different from being terrorized by a ghost. I was completely alone to face this. Being haunted is the loneliest situation a person can be in.

I wanted to find a way to stop it.

***

I had to live with the inevitable intrusion and would stay out of my room at night as late as possible. It seemed as if my fears were growing since I'd discovered the truth. Helpless to find a solution, each night became a test between the ghost and me. What did it want? It almost felt like the ghost wanted to be in the room because the specter kept coming back every night. Did it want me gone – want me out – want me to disappear?

School had started and I found it difficult to spend time away from my room when I was home. That was where I did homework and other projects. There was also a lot for me to worry about now, and I needed my refuge more than ever. When staying in the house, watching TV, or doing other things to avoid the ghost, I was always wishing to be out there.

The national news was grim, as usual. Even more disturbing were the reports about the Berkeley Free Speech Movement where 3,000 student activists at University of California blocked a police car from taking a volunteer who had been arrested for not showing his ID. The graphic videos on TV were frightening. The world that I lived in was in turmoil and the knowledge only added anxiety to my state of mind.

Avoiding going to my room only deprived me of the happiness of being in my own little space, the contentment to dream pleasantly and enjoy a newfound independence. Out there, I could contemplate the current issues of our nation, subjects that we talked about in school and concerns voiced amongst friends that muddled in my mind.

Looking elsewhere for contentment, in the cool evenings, I sometimes walked to enjoy the fresh air and clear my head. I loved the dark star-filled sky above and relished the joy of living. It was safe to walk through the old neighborhoods to the nearest corner store, a good turning point before heading back.

I stayed away as long as I could, but always, at some point, it was time to go back.

Once, returning from babysitting at 11:15 and very tired, I figured I'd missed the 11:00 o'clock visit so I hurried outside, through the dark courtyard toward my room. I opened the noisy outside door, my body tense as I walked through the two inky black storage rooms, my eyes searching the shadows before I closed the bedroom door behind me. Taking a shaky breath, I prepared for bed. That was when I heard a loud crash come from the direction of my parents' room.

I laid my head against the wall and listened as my dad yelled at mom. I knew he had hurt her again. I felt sick and angry but told myself that if it continued, I would go back inside the house. I would make him stop. It wouldn't be the first time I'd tried to make him stop. Even with his fist held up to my white, shaken face while he yelled, I had stood between him and mom. My stomach turned over as it always did when they were fighting. I was tense, afraid, and ready to go back inside the house.

I listened through the barrier. All was quiet on the other side of the wall. I felt the chill of anxiety that moved from my fingers and up my arms. I was terrified of my dad, and yet I could remember feeling the normal childish love that was what any daughter would feel for her father. The feelings were all mixed up inside of me, tangled with his abuse, his perversity, and extreme cruelty.

Suddenly, I heard loud footsteps outside my door that walked *away* from my room, through the two storage rooms, and as the outside door opened, the window rattled loudly and the door slammed shut!

The skin crawled all over my body as I realized that I must have walked past the ghost when I came in because it was waiting for me. It was inside – invisible – waiting. I knew I always heard the ghost come in – slam the door, stomp through the rooms, but after that, it simply disappeared. At least, that's what I thought.

Many times, I walked out there after 11:00 o'clock, after I was sure the ghost had already visited. I believed that it just disappeared – simply vanished after arriving at my bedroom door. No more noise – no more ghost.

This was the first time I ever heard the intruder *leave! It had been out there all the time when I walked through the rooms!* For the first time, it had left – had walked back with noisy boots, opened the noisy door and then slammed it shut, the loose window rattling loudly!

For the first time, I knew that now the ghost waited. Shivering, I sat on my bed as tears of fear gathered in my eyes. I wished I could go to my mom and tell her how scared I was, but she was in the house with dad, and he had probably hit her again. His bad temper had erupted again tonight – and the ghost had changed the usual routine – two things that terrified me!

***

This was a new routine for the ghost. Now when it came, after a noisy entrance, it stood outside my room for a period of time, then would walk out, boots banging on the floor through the two rooms before the noisy door opened and slammed shut. I had no idea what had changed the behavior, what had made the ghost linger now before brazenly leaving.

The intruder was beginning to affect me in many ways. I wondered about it a lot. Why was the ghost haunting? Why did the ghost come at the same time every night? Why did it suddenly change the routine and now, after coming in at 11:00 o'clock, and eventually disappearing, would now leave, walk out, and slam the door?

The question that bothered me the most was *why was I so scared*?

Most of my life, I had been a timid child, scared of many things. Maybe that was why I liked to read. A book always had an ending, and it usually resolved all the problems by the final chapter. Reading was safe and having my very own room to read in undisturbed was important to me. Now I had a ghost who was ruining that, and I was too frightened to confront it.

I believed the invisible being was more powerful than I was. It could do magic – appear and disappear, be invisible. It might be an evil ghost and harm me physically. I felt like a victim.

This was my first time to learn anything about a ghost. What little I'd ever heard or read had painted apparitions as frightening, terrifying and usually a product of imagination. I was not imagining this, and I was definitely scared!

***

My curiosity and desire to fix the problem prompted me to start asking questions about the house we lived in. Now that I knew it was a ghost, I wanted to find out who the specter was.

I didn't hesitate to knock on doors and ask my neighbors questions about who might have lived in the area the longest, someone who might have knowledge of the neighborhood. I finally found an old timer who lived nearby and had been in the neighborhood for many years.

I approached him as he worked in his garden. Since it was an older neighborhood, many residents were elderly folks. His yard was neat, clean and well cared for. After I told him who I was and where I lived, I asked, "Do you know how long our apartments have been there?"

The sun was unusually hot and its heat beat down on our heads. He laid his rake aside and answered, "Let me think. I think part of it was built before prohibition as a beer brewery and later converted to apartments."

"What about before that?"

"That's a long time ago, maybe as far back as the 1890's."

"Really?" For me to imagine this area that long ago was curious.

He shifted his stance and asked, "Why are you interested in that?"

"I'm just trying to find some history about our house."

"Don't your folks know?"

"No, we just bought it a while back, and we don't know much at all."

He rubbed his head before he put his hat back on. “I only know what’s been told around here. Not sure about the facts.”

A bee buzzed near my head, and I stepped aside while waving my hand to shoo it away. “That’s okay,” I was anxious for him to continue. “I’d like to learn anything.”

“An old story goes that there was a house that sat right there between the big trees before the brewery was built. That was a long time ago before anything was built out here. My family owned a farm up here,” he turned and pointed to a well-kept Victorian house. “That’s the original house. We kept it in the family until I bought it a long time ago. They sold off some land so other people could live here, too. I’ve been here most of my life.”

With interest, I asked, “You mean the old original house that was once on our lot, sat on that long side of the apartments, down where the big trees are on the side?”

I pointed to our place to verify my point. The view of our home was a little down below us since the houses were built on an incline.

“Yes, see that old apartment on the end? The side where the old fountains are standing, that’s where the house stood.”

I stared below at the Fountain Courts. That was where my bedroom was located. The second fountain stood in front of the apartment window of my bedroom.

I felt chills climb up my arms. The two huge trees in front of my room must have fronted the old house he was describing.

He continued, “The story went that the house belonged to an old man who lived alone.” He scratched his head, “He raised vegetables in a garden to support himself on land that he owned down there. As I've heard, he was a bit of a recluse and stayed away from people most of the time. He minded his own business and tended to his garden to sell the produce."

The man stepped into the shade of a nearby tree before he continued. "One night, a mysterious fire broke out in his house and it was assumed by everyone that he burned to death inside." He paused for a moment before he added, "He was never seen again. The only thing left was a deep old well beside the destroyed house that he had used to water his garden."

I said, "I don't think there's a well there now."

"No, I guess not. Things have changed."

A truck rattled by on the road by the garden. Dust lifted into the hot air and drifted.

"So what started the fire?" I asked.

"Now that's a good question. There were rumors that someone he once offended started the fire on purpose."

"You mean, someone killed him?"

"No one ever knew for sure."

He was quiet for a moment while he stared at our apartments. "A body was never found, but he was gone. No one saw him again."

I found my breath again and asked, "Did he have any family?"

The old man picked up his shovel before he answered, "Not that anyone ever knew of."

He started to walk away but suddenly turned back, "You know, that wasn't the only fire on that property. In the…let me think," he scratched his head. "Yes, about twenty-five years ago, I think around 1941, there was a fire at the Fountain Courts."

"Really? What happened?"

"I think a building in the courtyard burned."

"You mean, the bathhouse?"

"Yes! That was what it was called. Funny, I should remember that."

I thanked him and walked away, wondering if the missing vegetable grower might be my ghost.

Eerie

"Could I ever banish the memory of those haunted nights?"

The weather was turning cold and apartment number fifteen had no heat. In Idaho, winter can sneak up on you, so we were running out of time. My dad turned his attention to finding a way to warm my bedroom. The project of cutting out a door was postponed until he had more time.

Under our bigger, roomier family apartment, there was a cellar where we stored a bunch of stuff. It had cement walls that extended seven feet down, part of the outside three-foot foundation walls that ran the length of the building before plunging into the ground creating a cellar. The inside of the cellar ended right beneath my bedroom wall that separated apartment number fifteen from our family apartment. Dad had hoped it extended all the way and he could run heating ducts through to my bedroom. It was disheartening to discover a strong cement wall as a barrier.

Since number fifteen had the same three-foot foundation outside, he figured it should also have a cellar below. Deciding there must be a separate basement under there, he began to probe.

I was helping him scout things out, and we were both standing by the old outside door that led inside to my room. Dad started poking along the ground of the foundation, working up and feeling the boards that covered the side of the building.

"I know there's a way under there," he said while he worked. After a few minutes, he went inside and spent part of an hour searching for a trap door that would lead under the apartment. Having no luck, he returned outside and stood beside the cement foundation that was partially covered with the wood siding.

I offered, "Maybe they couldn't dig out a cellar here because of the roots of the big trees."

Ignoring me, he continued to examine the outside siding until finally he exclaimed, "Here it is!"

When he began to rip off the wooden siding boards, I wondered what he'd found. Clearing away a section, I could see he'd uncovered an old door in the wall that had been enclosed and hidden away. The siding on the outside of the old apartment had covered up the entrance. It was baffling to wonder why.

My dad shook his head, "This must be the cellar door. There has to be a reason they wanted to keep people out of here. Maybe it floods inside in the spring. Good thing its dry now so let's have a look."

When opened, it led down into the cellar. My dad reached up and ran his hand across the ceiling of the stairway above his head. "I bet this is hidden inside that storage closet in the old kitchen." He shook his head, "I looked in there the other day and it's so full of junk, I just closed the door. Who would have ever thought?"

He walked down the dirty steps, shining his flashlight as he moved forward. Reluctantly, I followed.

His light illuminated a cellar that was about the size of the old apartment. We were standing beneath my bedroom. There were shelves, now empty, that had once been used for storage. I imagine the brewery used it to store their brew. There were spider webs draped around and soft dirt an inch deep on the floor so I didn't moved very far inside.

I said, "It doesn't look like it floods in here."

He didn't answer as he shown his flashlight along a line of old wiring that ran across the roof. "That's what I'm looking for. A good power source."

He walked along the dirt floor following the cement wall as the wire snaked across the ceiling and into a dark hole. In that spot, the cement wall only went up about five feet, leaving an opening above that recessed further back. It resembled a crawl space and since that was where the wiring went, my dad went in search of a stepladder so he could crawl in there and follow the wiring.

Holding the flashlight, I stood on my toes and tried to peek into the opening but could see nothing as it was dark and musty in there. When he returned, he took the flashlight and crawled into the dark hole, sliding on his backside to fit into the small space.

Inside, the bottom was covered with old boards. His voice was muffled when he speculated, "I don't know what these boards are for. Covering the dirt, I guess."

I waited in the cellar with light shining from the open door into the dark space and worried that a spider might get on me. The more I stared at the webs, the more my skin crawled all over my body. When my dad hollered for me to get his hammer, I gladly obliged. Up the dirty steps I went, in search of his toolbox. The fresh air and sunshine was rejuvenating and I took my time.

When I returned, he was jumping out from the hole, mumbling to himself as he moved. "What the – !" He stood on the ladder, shining his light onto the rotted boards that he'd just been laying on. "Look at that! They broke away and nearly took me with them!"

"What happened?"

"There's a hole under the boards!" He leaned in and shone the light down as he gazed. "Wow, that's a deep hole. It looks like an old well! It must be 30 feet deep." After a few moments, he stepped down and brushed off his clothes. He was shaken and disturbed.

"No water in it – just a deep hole with debris at the bottom. No one said anything about a well being here when I bought this place." His face was flushed and his eyes were bright with emotion. "Go on, look at it!"

I was taken aback, because the last thing on earth I wanted to do was to lean up into that dark hole and look at something that might be a creepy old well.

"Go on! You won't fall!"

Because he was so insistent that I substantiate his findings, I took the flashlight and crawled up the ladder. I leaned over and saw the disturbed boards, some broken away. When I shined the light down, I could see a wall that was rounded and bricked at the top. I had to lean further in for my light to follow the circular brick and rock wall down to the bottom of the empty well. It was deep and I instantly felt vertigo grab hold of me. I jumped back and stepped down the ladder, my hand shaking when I handed him the flashlight.

He said, "I was almost lying at the bottom." His head nodded as anger settled in his expression, "I think I'll call the previous owners and ask them about this."

We left the cellar without finishing checking out the wiring. My dad was irate at what had happened and went into the house. I returned to my room.

I didn't tell him what the old man had told me about the well that had once been located on this property. Could this be the same well? Why would it be boarded up with an apartment built on top of it? If it had been dug as a well at the same time the beer brewery was built, it would have been outside in the yard – right?

Thoughtfully, I speculated about the fact that the old well really existed and was hidden beneath my apartment area. In fact, it was actually directly beneath the outer room, the one next to my room, the one that I would hear the heavy footsteps walk through every night.

Later on, when I went back into the house, dad was talking to mom about the well. "They said they had no idea there was an old well under the apartment. It's not in the property description. In fact, this is the first anyone has heard of it."

He was still angry that he'd come so close to being hurt by something that was never disclosed to him when he purchased the property.

***

Early that evening, Cheryl came out to visit me and brought her old boyfriend, Don with her. He'd heard about the well and wanted me to tell him what happened.

After I explained the incident to him, I decided to trust him with the whole story. "There's an elderly man who lives up on the hill who told me about an old well that was on our property." I shared all I knew.

Don said, "If there was ever a well built here then there is a record of it. The county keeps track of that stuff. It should have been recorded on the deed, but it sounds like that wasn't done."

He promised to look into it.

It was comforting to have someone else believe in what was happening to me – the footsteps that I was hearing and especially the distress it was bringing into my life. I'm sure that Don was anxious to help resolve this situation if he could. He wanted to stay friends with Cheryl.

I know that my friend Steve believed me and many times, I wanted him to come back over and help investigate. He had been gone for a week at the end of summer, staying with his cousins out of town. After school started, he was always busy with sports and his evening job at the theater.

As I prepared for bed that night, I had many things to think about. It was cold in my room, and I didn't know when my dad would work on getting heat in there again. School was in full progress – my senior year, and it was a busy time. There was something unsettling about knowing it was the last year of school, a wrapping up of twelve long years, a final stamp on a section of life enveloped and centered on the environment of formal education; a perimeter that would soon disappear, and be replaced by – what?

For a girl graduating from school in 1965, the future was obscure. Girls were not expected to have a career; they were expected to get married and have a family. To choose to have a career was a more difficult path because opportunities were limited. The anticipated income level was nominal compared to that of men who had families to support. A woman should be home, raising children.

Usually a war could change how women functioned in our society, shouldering more than their share of male-oriented jobs and proving their true strength. As history proved, when WWII expanded, the changing role of women who suddenly and successfully shouldered male-oriented jobs became evident.

I wanted to go to college and do more than just get married. I wanted to have exciting adventures, supporting myself by doing something I loved.

My folks tentatively ignored what I wanted, as if I was just a daydreamer. College was expensive. They made it clear that if that was what I wanted, then I would have to do it on my own – get a job, save my money, and pay for college. If I was adult enough to want to follow ambitions, then I was adult enough to make it happen.

Our options were shifting. The boys who graduated from High School in 1965 might soon be marching off to war. Planning to get married, after graduation, involved the specter of the U.S. Military peeking over your shoulder and deciding the destiny of your mate. The future looked bleak.

I had my share of boyfriends, but nothing serious enough to lead up to marriage. My priorities were to go to college, have a career, and then maybe think about marriage.

I snuggled deep into my warm bed, waiting for my toes to warm up. The leaves outside had dropped from the big lilac bushes and lay scattered across the ground. Only the bare branches remained, reaching for the sky. I could see the moon buried in the skeletal arms of the trees as its light glowed behind the black limbs. I glanced at my clock and it was time – time for the ghost to come.

Spectral

"I think he whispers terror to my soul – 'wake-up!"

I had never repaired the latch lock on my bedroom door, so it would always stand open a few inches. For some unexplained reason, the door seemed to lean on its hinges now, as one hinge was loosened and almost unattached. It would no longer close all the way shut. When I mentioned it to my dad, he was irritable and told me he would get to it when he had time.

I looped a string from the portion of the broken hook still left on the doorframe to wrap around a nail that I drove into the door. No one could walk into my room unless I unhooked it. At least I could dress in privacy without one of my sisters or my parents walking in on me.

Finally falling asleep after the visit by the ghost, my body shaking and my nerves racked, doubts began to grow about my lack of courage that could turn out to be a true character flaw. Normally, I considered myself to be a dare devil, but in this instance, I had no backbone whatsoever.

It was well past midnight when I woke again. In fact, it was just a few minutes before 1 a.m. I lay in bed and listened to the wind howl outside. In October, it was too early for snow, but sometimes Mother Nature surprised us.

I burrowed deeper into the covers, while the cold nipped at my cheeks. Just as I began to doze, I was shocked to hear the outside door rattle open, slam shut and the heavy footsteps walk across the floor before stopping just on the other side of my bedroom door. This time I was truly afraid because the ghost never came at this hour! He had already come at 11:00. This must be someone else. *This must be a real person!*

I had no way to defend myself, and my only defense was to lie still, hardly breathing, and pray. After a few minutes, the steps sounded loudly and walked away before the outer door slammed shut. It was gone.

Who was it – the ghost or a real person? I reached over and turned on my bed lamp. The room looked normal and the light seemed to reassure me. If it was my sister, she would have come in. Maybe she changed her mind. Nevertheless, the footsteps – those were the steps of the ghost!

After a sleepless night, I hurried to school the next day. Feeling distracted all day long, when I went home, I decided to tell my folks again, what I was hearing at night. The intrusion at 1 a.m. worried me. It might be something else.

Mom was cooking dinner and listened to me at the same time as she listened to some music she was curious to learn. She was an accomplished pianist, a natural *savant* and played only "by ear", perfectly duplicating anything she heard. She had built a professional career from her talent.

She played her first tune on the old family organ when she was just three years old. By the time she was twelve, she was the organist in church every Sunday until she left home. When she was eleven, she played weekly in a band with her dad and brothers for local dances. Since they were farmers and lived in a farming community, these dances were attended by families from far and near. Music was in her bones, and she could interpret it so well that others fell in love with music, too.

As I rambled on, she smiled and cocked her head as she listened to the tricky notes in the song. She'd lost her hearing in one ear many years ago after a brutal beating from my dad.

"Peach blossom, this is an old house. There are lots of funny noises. Don't worry so much about peculiar bumps in the night. You're safe."

When my dad came home, Mom hurried to get dinner on the table. I waited until he had eaten before I told him what happened last night. I was afraid that this new intruder might be someone else. Even though it sounded exactly like the ghost, he had never come twice in one night.

Dad stood up and noisily pushed his chair against the wall. When he was angry, his eyes flashed hot color.

He yelled, "I don't want to hear about shenanigans your friends are up to! So help me, if I catch them, they'll be sorry!" He walked to his gun cabinet and reached inside. Pulling out a rifle, he carried it to the couch and began to cock the gun, checking inside for bullets.

Whenever he got out his guns, it frightened me. I had terrifying memories from my childhood about the guns, times when he had been angry. Especially the time he held the barrels to our heads, threatening to pull the trigger if we ever told.

I started to help mom clean up but she shooed me away, the fear in her eyes reflecting mine. She whispered, "You better get your homework done."

All these many years later, I know that my dad must have suffered from a severe case of PTSD. After his years of service in WWII, his horrific experiences in Europe – being shot by the enemy, robbed by a fellow comrade as he lay wounded, and then left for dead – he was burdened with fear and anger that was buried deep inside him. He was awarded the Purple Heart for his bravery, but we felt the brunt of the residue for years. On top of all that, his childhood carried scars that twisted his mind. He was an intelligent man but trauma had turned him into a monster.

I hesitated to leave Mom inside with my dad, but she assured me she would be fine. I was glad to go out to my room. I was safer out there, than I was in the house. Even though there was a ghost who wanted me to get out, I was determined to stay. It was my only refuge.

I pulled out my diary and began to pour out my heart. Writing down what was happening to me was a comfort. After I finished, I hid it inside my drawer because I didn't want anyone to read my inner thoughts.

Concentrating on homework was difficult, but I had to finish. The pressure to get good grades, especially as a senior, was heavy on my shoulders. The report I was writing was about recent events that included Martin Luther King, Jr., a leader in the American civil rights movement who was, just this month, awarded the Nobel Peace Prize.

Finally finished and exhausted, I crawled into bed.

Sleep was almost instant, until I was dragged awake by the opening of the noisy outside door, the heavy footsteps, and the many minutes it lingered outside my door before it left. I couldn't help the tears that streamed from my eyes, the helpless sobs that chocked inside me when I glanced at my clock and saw the time was 11 o'clock.

Squelching the fear that wanted to overcome me, I eventually fell asleep again. My dreams were filled with confusion where nothing made any sense – a lot like the story of Alice in Wonderland, the queer characters, the unusual happenstance, and the peculiar reasoning.

I almost didn't realize that I was awake when my eyes suddenly focused on the clock next to my bed. It was 1 a.m. and something woke me up. I turned on my side, hugging the edge of the bed, leaving the other half of the full bed empty. I didn't want to wake up and worry, but the sounds of the night seeped into my head. I began to replay my day inside my mind. I listened as a night bird called out and I could hear something scurry inside my closet. It was most likely a mouse. They seemed to come inside when winter was on the way. I glanced at my door, the string loop in place while a dark gap showed where the door wouldn't close properly.

Very slowly and quietly, I could hear soft breathing behind me. I lay still on my side and sharpened my ears.

I knew I was alone in my room. No one else was there.

I had never heard this sound coming through the wall between my room and the house before. The walls were thick and even when my parents were fighting, I could never hear the words. This was different.

Was it coming through the wall? No, it was behind me, as I lay on my side, my back turned against the other side of the bed.

It was obviously someone breathing and it was getting louder and louder. I could almost feel the air move against my back because it was right next to me! *Lying next to me on the bed!* The breathing was loud, as it seemed to hover close to me, as if against my ear. I felt no physical pressure, just the constant sound of a soul breathing.

I have never panicked in my life as I did at that moment. I wasn't able to take a breath myself and could only hear the loud, heavy breaths of someone beside me. All I had to do was turn over in the bed to see who it was. That's all I had to do, just roll aside and open my eyes!

The blood pounded in my head. What would I see? Would it be human? Would it be white like a ghost or would it be some murky green color? What would happen after I looked at it? What would it do?

If it could breathe, then it was real – in some timeless misunderstood sense – it was more than just a ghost. The most disturbing thought of all was the idea that it had come into my room! It no longer stayed on the other side of the door.

I lay there as the breathing became louder and steadier. *What was wrong with me? Why couldn't I look?* It wasn't the wind, because I'd never heard wind that sounded like that. My window was closed and there was no wind tonight. It wasn't coming from the house on the other side of the wall because the sound was right behind me! There was no other explanation about what it was, even though I was frantic to find something to attribute to the sound.

I was shaking hard as the breathing started to slowly fade until it stopped. There were no sounds and all was quiet. I licked my dry lips and unclasped my balled up hands. I was disgusted with myself because I had been unable to turn over in bed and see whatever it was.

I thought of the cellar and the discovery of the deep old well. What if, at the bottom of that well, there are the remains of a body – only a skeleton by now, but forever forgotten; by uncovering the well, we had disturbed a grave. I shook my head to clear the vision. Right now, my imagination was definitely working overtime!

Suddenly and impulsively, I jumped up and ran through the dark outer rooms, opened the noisy outside door and raced through the dark courtyard into the house. The terror I felt was indescribable!

The couch in the living room was my bed for the rest of the night.

***

I could smell coffee brewing. My dad enjoyed coffee at home on Saturday morning. When I finally opened my eyes, I saw my sister, Tyke, sitting at the end of the couch by my feet. She was curled up in a blanket.

"Hi," I said.

"What are you doing on the couch?" she asked.

Tyke was only a year and a half younger than I was. We were close and enjoyed not only a sisterhood, but also a close friendship.

I glanced around to see where my dad was. Her eyes followed mine and she whispered, "He's outside, packing the boat."

I rolled my eyes and asked, "Do we have to go again? It's getting too cold to camp." Hopefully, this would be one of the last trips for the year.

"Yes, Dad says it's still warm enough. Better hurry," she jumped off the couch and ran into her room.

My older sister, Cheryl, didn't have to go on the boat trips anymore because she was married. Only Tyke and I were still stuck going with our parents. My dad loved to fish and he never minded the freezing weather as long as he had a pole in his hand. He made sure we had a warm tent with a heater to huddle around. My mom was happy to support his outdoor activities and knew how to cook delicious fresh trout in the wild.

I got up, followed my sister to her room and watched her gather her stuff together. "I'll help you if you'll come help me." I was hesitant to go out to my room alone.

She said, "Sure, I'll help, but you have to tell me why you were on the couch this morning."

Nervously, I answered, "If anyone else wants to know, my room was cold so I came in to sleep."

She eagerly sat beside me and breathlessly asked, "Tell me what really happened!"

We finished packing her weekend bag and then went out to my room. In the morning daylight, it looked normal. We both stood at the end of the bed, and I felt goose bumps rise across my arms.

Tyke whispered, “Are you sure it wasn’t the wind?”

“Positive. Listen, it’s blowing out there right now, and what do you hear?”

She listened for a moment, “No, doesn’t sound like breathing to me.”

“Me, either; there’s no doubt about what it was.”

Tyke commented, “It’s weird – happening right after you guys found the old well.”

I didn’t answer as I pulled out my overnight bag and began to pack enough stuff for a weekend of camping.

She continued, “Do you think there could have been any air blowing or wind coming from the well?”

I stopped what I was doing and considered what she suggested. “I think dad covered it up again with new boards. I saw mom putting some storage down there, too.”

Tyke said, “We should check it out, you know, go down there and see what we can hear. See if something sounds like breathing.”

For the first time, I considered that maybe what I’d heard last night had an explanation. Maybe there wasn’t a ghost lying beside me in my bed. Maybe there was a perfectly logical explanation about it. Happily, I answered, “Yes! You’re right! We should.”

I watched my dad outside the window as he returned to the front of the house. "We'll have to wait 'til we get back. Then we can go down there."

We stared at each other, and I asked, "Do we have to go at night?"

"No, we can check in the daytime, don't you think?"

I nodded my head, envisioning myself down in the cellar after dark. "Yes – daylight only!"

Ceaseless

Revised diary entry dated November – December 1964

We returned from the camping trip late Sunday afternoon, and the next day was back to school. The week was a busy one as we moved into November. It was a while before Tyke and I were able to explore the cellar.

I slept in my sister's room for the first few nights after we came home. Not wanting to face my room alone, I stayed in the house. The news that evening was about controversy over the possible approval of Lyndon B. Johnson's nomination as the presidential elect for the Democratic Party. I wasn't thinking about politics or even the most recent nuclear device detonated inside the Tatum Salt Dome, in Mississippi. After all, in elementary school we practiced nuclear bomb attack procedures on a regular basis. Scrambling under our desks when the alarm sounded, we shielded our heads with our arms, as if that was any kind of protection from an A-bomb. Still our brains were programed to face the worst.

This time, I was thinking of my room.

As the memory of the harrowing experience of lying alone in bed – listening to an entity breath next to me – began to soften, I told myself, it must have been a strange wind blowing up from the well.

Returning to my room, I made sure to latch the door with my humble string. I noticed the door hung more lopsided than before and after investigating, I found that the bottom hinge was completely broken away from the frame. Only one hinge at the top was holding the door. *When did that happen?* As a precaution, I moved a heavily padded wooden sofa chair in front of the door to make sure no one could push it open.

Even though I would have liked my dad to fix the broken hinge, I didn't dare mention it. For some reason whenever the holidays started to approach, he became angrier and angrier. It was best to avoid him if possible during that time – one lesson I'd learned early in my life. My mom wasn't able to avoid it though, and during most holidays, she ended up bruised and battered.

I could still see the look in my dad's eyes the last time I stood between them during a terrible fight. She was horrified for me, but he finally stepped away, the expression on his face promising me that if I did that again, I would suffer the consequences.

After school was out one day, Tyke and I went down into the cellar. The sun was still up but getting dim as twilight came early this time of year. We each carried a flashlight.

The bug population was down by now as cold weather drove them into all the nooks and crannies. The spiders still flourished and I shone my light across the ceiling looking for dangling webs.

There was a light down there by now, as my dad had installed one before he began the work to cover the old well with new solid boards. He planned to have the whole thing filled with cement to prevent any future mishaps.

I found the light switch and turned it on. Bright light flooded the room and it no longer held any threats in its shadows. The cobwebs and dirt had been swept away and carefully cleaned by mom.

Relief sounded in my voice when I said, "That's much better."

We stood beside each other, staring around at the shelves now filled with food storage, canned dry goods ordered from a company who promised it would last for many years and still taste delicious. We picked through the food to see if anything looked good.

Tyke commented, "Did you notice how hard the wind was blowing outside before we came down here?"

I nodded. We stood still and listened; the silence was almost unnerving, it was so quiet. Stepping over to the location where the well lay behind the half cement wall, we could see the ends of thick new boards that now covered it. There was no wind blowing inside this sheltered cellar and deep well beneath my apartment. The old well was silent and kept its secrets.

My tone was soft when I lamented, "The well isn't breathing. You know what that means?" I sighed, "I wonder why the ghost haunts? What does it want?"

My sister offered, "It wants everyone to go away."

"Yes, I think so, too, but why? I just want my own room and for it to leave me alone." I looked above my head and raised my voice, "*Why won't you leave me alone*?"

No one said anything as we both almost expected an answer. Tyke suggested, "The next time it comes, you should open your door and ask!"

I shivered, "I can't. Why don't you come and stay with me some night and you can ask?"

She quickly responded, "No – I'm never gonna stay there! It's too scary for me!"

We both heard the loud sounds of someone coming into the cellar. Cheryl called out, "Hey, are you down here?"

She stepped into the room with her old boyfriend, Don following her. "What are you doing?"

"Just looking around."

"Don has some news."

I said, "Let's go upstairs."

We all went into my room and found places to sit comfortably. Don stood near Cheryl as she lay across the bed while I sat beside her and Tyke.

Cheryl said, "Remember when you asked Don to check into the existence of the well?" She looked up at him.

Don said, "I checked the records kept in the county offices, and there was a well located on this property. It was in the late 1800's and was used for residential and commercial gardening purposes. So, it's true that someone lived here and grew vegetables to sell."

I was excited to learn this because it gave substance to some of the bizarre occurrences now happening. It also supported the story told by my elderly neighbor about the vegetable farmer who once lived here. "That means that the rest of the story – about him burning to death – could also be true."

Tyke said, "That's why he's a ghost!"

Cheryl asked, "Why were you down in the cellar?"

After I told the story of the ghostly breathing that had occurred, the silence in the room was thick. Cheryl rubbed her arms as if chilled, before she stood up and said, "We better go."

I thanked Don for his help, and he promised to see if he could find out anything about a vegetable farmer who lived here and may have burned to death.

Tyke also went back into the house. I tried to coax her to stay. "Why don't you stay out here tonight?"

Her eyes were large when she answered, "No way. Too creepy out here for me!"

I was left alone in my room. By now, it was dark outside, and I was anxious about the facts that were falling into place that might explain the nightly visits. Reaching for my diary, I faithfully recorded my thoughts.

***

"Dear Diary,

...It feels so wonderful to have a few people who believe me and want to help. This can't be the first time a ghost ever haunted, although it is the first time for me! I keep thinking that if I can find out what the ghost wants from me, then it will go away. Isn't that logical? I mean, it wouldn't be here if it didn't want something, maybe to give a message to a loved one, or to share a secret before it can leave? I don't get a good feeling from this ghost, though. I'm happy in my room until it comes and ruins it. I feel terrified and so afraid! That doesn't sound like a good ghost to me..."

I knew very little about ghosts or why they haunted, but this ghost was becoming personal with me. It was a chilling thought to wonder why something from another realm picked me to communicate whatever it was it needed to say.

That night I was too wound up to relax or fall asleep before the dreaded hour rolled around. My ears were sharp as I listened for the usual sounds that preceded the visit. Whenever I remembered the deep, heavy breaths that I'd heard before, my stomach would knot into a tight ball. I turned in the bed to face the empty side. This time I would see where the breathing came from.

The silence was only softened by the wind outside that relentlessly pushed a young branch back and forth across the side of the house. What sound would I hear tonight; maybe, the door rattling, the heavy footsteps, and the deep breath beside me? I swallowed the lump that had formed in my throat.

At 11:00 o'clock, the outside door opened noisily, the loud footsteps walked through the two dark rooms before the entity stood just on the other side of my bedroom door. Through the moonlight that filtered from the window, I stared at the doorway. The string was latched across the strong nail; the hefty chair was pushed against the solid wood front of the door. I glanced for a moment at the other side of my bed, the pillow that lay undisturbed, with covers up against it.

For a moment, panic began to mount inside of me. I'm sure my eyes bulged. All the thoughts that raced inside my head of the possibilities of what could happen, were overwhelming, so I closed my eyes and waited. I heard the heavy steps walk away, the outer door slam, the window rattle loudly.

Thankful that it was gone, I fell into a deep troubled sleep. It seemed as if I'd just closed my eyes when suddenly I was wide-awake again. The clock read 1:00 o'clock. I heard the ghost return, slam the door, stomp through the rooms before it eventually left.

I sat up, my mind burning with questions. I'd heard the footsteps at 1:00 o'clock before, and at that time, wondered if they belonged to someone else. Then I'd heard the breathing at 1:00 o'clock. Now I heard the entity come with its usual commotion at the same time.

I knew that the ghost had a new routine. It came at 11:00 o'clock and returned at 1:00 o'clock and was becoming bolder.

***

November was slipping by, and the problems that all adolescents experienced were surrounding me. A quarter of my senior year was close to being over, and there was no way to stop the march of time.

My sister Cheryl came into my room one day with Don beside her. She asked, "Do you have a minute? Don had an idea."

Don looked around my room and said, "I think all this strange stuff that is happening might have an explanation. I had an idea, but you might think I'm crazy…"

I asked, "What?"

He continued, "Did you know there is a group of people at Idaho State University who investigate ghost hauntings?"

"I've never heard of such a thing. There are people who do that?"

"That's what I've been told. What would you think if I asked them to come over here and look into everything that is happening here?"

"I would love that!"

Cheryl asked, "What do you think dad would say?"

Disheartened, I answered, "He'd never let that happen."

"We could ask."

I shook my head. I knew my dad would flip out at something like that going on in his house. "He won't let us do that."

Don knew the situation in our home with our family. He was not only Cheryl's ex-boyfriend, but he also worked with my mom in the music world. He was a great drummer who did part-time gigs to help pay his tuition at school. He knew about some of the abuse suffered by my mom because Cheryl had told him when they were dating.

He said, "Let me talk to them and see what they say. Maybe we can do it sometime when your dad is gone."

For me, this was something I was yearning for – someone who might make the ghost go away; someone who believed that I was telling the truth and still wanted to help!

***

Each night, the clock would approach the ghostly hour and I couldn't stop it. Each night I listened for the heavy breathing when *something* was beside me in my bed – something invisible, not of this earth, and yet able to make sounds as if it was real; something that still reached out every night, approaching my door, trying to tell me something. I listened for it, but the deep, loud breathing I'd once heard was silent.

In my mind, I was retracing the area of the cellar, like drawing a map. Where exactly did the well sit beneath my apartment? When I remembered the awkward space below, the cement part of a wall where the well lay on the other side, tucked away and forgotten, I realized the space below didn't match the space above. I didn't know how it was off – I just knew it was.

Out in my room, I walked around and noticed that my apartment was shaped like a stubby, backward "L", laid on its side. The long arm connected to the house and the little hook that pointed southward was the kitchen nook, where the door with the loose window led outside into the courtyard.

The cellar had a different shape. It was a small square, like a slimmer version of the upstairs. If I remembered correctly, the well sat beneath the kitchen nook that extended out a bit. Because the wall had been cemented partway up in the cellar, the nook was disguised and partly hidden, so that the nook below was invisible. That made the cellar room a thin rectangle. It just seemed to be so much smaller than the upstairs.

Wondering if my mind was playing tricks on me, I reasoned that it would be a good idea to measure both spaces and see if they matched. The cellar with the old well was a part of the history of this property and could hold a clue to the mystery of the haunting.

Saturday had finally come and I went into the house to look for my sister. Dad was gone and mom was cleaning in her room. I found Tyke in her bedroom.

I said, "Tyke, come with me." She followed, knowing that I must have something serious on my mind.

We went into the cellar.

She asked, "What are we doing down here?"

I held up the tape measurer, "We need to measure the room and I want you to hold the end of the tape."

"Why?"

"You'll see."

Carefully, we measured each wall. Some had shelves and were more difficult to maneuver around, but each detail was written down and a rough diagram was drawn that somewhat resembled the cellar.

When we were finished, I said, "Now, let's go upstairs and measure the rooms."

"Not until you tell me why we're doing this."

As we climbed the steps out of the cellar, I answered, "I think there is something off. I don't know what, but I just have a feeling."

"What kind of feeling?"

"I don't know. Like there's a question that needs an answer."

"Huh?"

"Never mind; let's finish."

We went upstairs and measured each room of apartment fifteen; first, the small kitchen, then the living room and finally my bedroom. The two rooms weren't cleaned like the cellar or my room. Used only for storing miscellaneous items of furniture, boxes and various building supplies, it was dusty and contained remnants of spider webs. After much anguish and fear about seeing a bug, we finished.

Sitting comfortably on the bed in my room, we compared the upstairs and downstairs measurements.

Puzzled, I said, "It doesn't match."

"Maybe we measured wrong."

My frustration was probably echoed in my voice, "We were careful! But maybe we made a mistake. Let's do it again."

Tyke frowned, "Do we have to?" She brushed her soiled hands against her pants. "I feel so dirty."

My hands were dirty, too. "Come on, let's get it over with."

We quickly redid the upstairs and it matched our previous measurements. Going back into the cellar, the dimensions once again matched our prior amounts.

"It looks like this space down here is smaller than upstairs."

Tyke asked, "What part doesn't match?"

I walked around the room, examining the walls and comparing it with the diagram I'd drawn of the upstairs. "This wall is off. You know, upstairs where the old bathroom was that I now use as a closet? That whole wall is about four feet smaller down here."

"Your closet isn't that big. It's tiny."

"I know."

We walked over to the cement wall and stared at it. It was about fifteen feet long and sat in a room that measured twelve feet wide, whereas upstairs it measured much wider. That meant that a portion of this basement was hidden behind this floor to ceiling cement wall. The width was off from the upstairs by several feet. I knew that the old, hidden well accounted for part of that footage; but what about the rest of the room? Why would anyone cover several feet of valuable storage space and make it inaccessible for use of any kind by erecting a solid cement wall?

We went back into the house and cleaned ourselves up. Neither one of us had an answer to the reason for the hidden space behind the cement wall. When I went out through the courtyard and into my room, I walked around, thinking that beneath my feet lay the hidden room, a dark, black room that no one knew about. What secrets did it conceal?

The Secret Room

"I'm afraid to see what's in the dark..."

Close to Thanksgiving, I decided I should ask my dad about the room hidden in the cellar. I had stopped telling my parents anything about the occurrences that happened nightly. They had a way of making the ordeal into something that was my fault – my fault for having friends who probably played tricks on me – my fault for having a big imagination – then there was always the threat of losing my room. I wanted to keep my sanctuary!

Don had moved out of his apartment so I didn't hear any more about the ghost investigators and felt completely alone during this trial.

Not only did I have the mystery of the ghost on my mind, I was also sewing a new dress for the upcoming prom, plus working on reports for school assignments.

Each night I had to endure the strange visits in the dark, always trying to find the courage to confront the ghost. I was such a coward and berated myself for being like that. There were so many other ways that I was brave, but this seemed to continue to terrify and render me witless.

I pretended to just be curious when I told my dad about the hidden room. I showed him the measurements Tyke and I had made. He went into the cellar and saw for himself that it was unaccountable space that was inaccessible. When I asked him if he could make a hole in the wall so that we could see inside, he laughed at me. He didn't care what was in there and said there was probably a good reason it was cemented up.

I asked, "Can me and Tyke make a hole there in the wall?"

"That's cement! You could never make a hole."

After he left, I found my sister and told her we should try to make a hole in the wall and peek inside.

"How do we do that?" she asked.

"Let's figure it out."

We raided my dad's tool chest and found a couple hammers and chisels. Then we went looking for someone to help us. After promising to pay a couple of younger boys from the neighborhood, they began to hammer the chisels against the cement. After a half hour, they left and said it was impossible.

Tyke suggested, "We just need stronger boys."

For the next week, we cajoled and bullied and begged anyone who could help us break into the wall. It was cold in the cellar and not too many guys wanted to work for very long. Progress was slow and to our horror, the wall was thick – at least six inches of pure concrete. We were working on creating a hole in the middle of the wall, right at eyesight level. As the chips slowly peeled away, the hole appeared more concave each day, until finally one day, we broke through to the other side!

There was only a tiny hole about the size of a finger, but on the other side was air – black and dark, but at least no more concrete!

We lost all of our help that day because they had fulfilled their part by making a tiny hole to the other side. From then on, we were the only ones who worked on the wall. We couldn't see anything through the hole, so we knew we had to make it bigger.

Later, I wondered if making that hole in the wall somehow affected the ghost in some confusing way. The air in my room felt heavier and almost stifling. In the evening, after I latched the string on the broken door – the one hinge still in place and holding on admirably – I settled into bed to wait for the first visit. The sound of the rattling door seemed louder, the footsteps harder, the sense of a presence on the other side of the door, much stronger. An intense energy pervaded the space in my room and seemed to settle in, dragging my spirits down and blanketing the joy I once felt.

***

Snow had begun to fall as winter set in. Since I still had no heat in my room, I used a small space heater. It was cozy in there, the bedside lamps shown cheerily, as my shelf of books stood neat and tidy beside the desk that I used for schoolwork and writing. My dad said I should move into the house until he could finish getting heat into my room, but I opted to stay out in my own space.

I turned on the radio and listened as a newsperson talked about rumors that President Johnson was considering a plan to bomb North Vietnam. It sounded as if the war was ramping up and some of my friends could be lost to it. I felt as if I belonged to a doomed generation.

This day was Saturday and my sister and I were determined to finish making the hole in the wall large enough to shine a flashlight inside the black space. That kind of hard labor was perfect for a cold winter day.

Even though our hands were freezing, we chipped and scraped for a few hours until the hole was about a two inch circumference and we could shine a light inside. Since it was so small, our big flashlight blocked the view.

"Hold it here, further out so that only the light shines inside and I can peek in there," I instructed my sister. My head kept blocking the light and I stretched awkwardly to see.

"What do you see?" she kept asking.

With such a limited viewing area, I could only see empty space. When I angled the light just right, I could see something bulky in the center of the room.

"There's something in there!" Excited, we began to chip at the cement in an effort to make the tiny hole bigger.

Tyke said, "Wonder what you saw? What did it look like?"

"I think it was a stool. You know, the kind that sits on three long legs, but a tall one, like for a person to sit at a counter or something."

"A stool?"

"Maybe, just not sure."

After taking a break for lunch and to rest our sore arms, we went back to work. The little hole grew bigger as we continued to hammer away with our chisels. We wanted to make it big enough to put our flashlight inside and see better, but that would require a lot more work. The flashlight was big and bulky with large heavy batteries.

We were exhausted and decided to continue in the morning. We had been working at this nearly all day and our arms were sore from the continued hammering.

That night, I slept hard and was only half-awake when the ghost came for the first visit. Jerking from sleep, the blood rushed into my head as my arms tingled with tiny hairs that rose. I listened to the frightful sounds as the door slammed and the heavy footsteps stomped across the two rooms. I waited, wondering what would happen next – maybe something more frightening. I listened as it left, slamming the door.

Later that night, in the haze of sleepy awareness, I thought I heard something slide across the floor in my room.

I bolted awake, my heart pounding, my breathing heavy. Everything was quiet. I looked around and that was when I noticed that my door was unlatched. Had I forgotten to fasten it when I went to bed? I had been so tired, I could have, but that was a habit ingrained into my head so strongly that I never forgot. At least the big, heavy chair was there in its place blocking the doorway. I looked at the clock and it said the time was 1:00 a.m.

I crawled out of bed and hooked the string over the nail on the door. That was when I saw that the antique footstool that always stood in a corner behind the dressing screen, was sitting right in the middle of the floor. I never moved it from its corner. I walked over and pushed it back. The sound it made was just like the noise that woke me.

Suddenly goose bumps rose across my arms and I leaped back into bed. It was deathly quiet in my room and I wondered if the ghost had come yet. Something had moved the footstool and I knew I'd heard the sound. It had to be the ghost. Was it in here right now?

I was unable to sleep after that as I continued to listen to all the sounds. There was no wind and the new snow covered noise from outside, while the only sound from above was of creaking wood that every house makes in its old age. Finally, I slept.

The next day, in spite of sore muscles, my sister and I were back at work on the hole in the wall. By the time lunch had passed, we'd made a larger hole and could shine our light inside *plus* clearly see what was in there.

The room was bare except for the three-legged stool that stood in the center of the space. Above it, hung a light bulb that dangled from a wire that dropped down from the ceiling. Beside the stool, there was a large duffle bag on the floor partially bulked up with contents. Everything was covered with many layers of dust, but not a single footprint of any living animal on the floor. On a far wall near the end, was the old sewer pipe that dropped down from the defunct bathroom above that now served as my closet. The rest of the room was clean, not a bit of junk anywhere, except for the oversized bag. It was a mystery.

***

"Dear Diary,

...We found a secret room in the cellar. It has a tall stool in there with a light bulb that hangs above. On the floor is a big duffle bag, like the one that the men carry in war, and it is half-full of something – can't tell what. It looks like it's a sort of green color or maybe brown. The stool is an old-fashioned stool used by old time shopkeepers. There is nothing else in there, just dirt everywhere. We shined our light in every corner and they are bare. I want to see what's in the bag. Why would something like that be hidden behind a cement wall? What purpose could that serve – unless the bag had a dead body in it and it smelled. They could have just buried it somewhere. Maybe the bag is full of money! Or gold! Why bury it behind a cement wall? Why leave a perfectly good stool inside. What does the hanging light bulb mean? Was someone buried alive and could only see until the bulb burned out?

I have so many questions and no answers! I'm so anxious to solve the mystery about why my ghost haunts because when I do, maybe it will go away..."

***

Why would anyone go to all the trouble of cementing a wall around this room? What was the purpose of closing it off and hiding it from everyone? Why make a six-inch thick concrete wall that ran floor to ceiling?

We needed to make the hole large enough to get inside and investigate what was in that old duffle bag. If someone had been trying to hide a body, it would be easier to have carried it into the yard and dug a hole, then to set it inside a thick cement wall. Why leave the three-legged stool with the duffle bag beside it on the floor inside the walled up room? What was inside the duffel bag? What did the secret room have to do with the haunting of the ghost upstairs? Was there a connection?

Mysteries

"It walks at night and nothing I do will stop the ghost…"

Time passed swiftly after that. Tyke got sick with the flu so we postponed our wall chipping until she was better. The Christmas holiday and all its' activities drew close. One evening, I felt restless, as if there was something significant about to happen. The sun had been hampered in its efforts to shine all day long by winter clouds permanently settled against the hills that surrounded the valley.

The world outside was a winter wonderland with frost covered branches and a few crisp, frozen leaves that still clung to forlorn branches. It was twilight and cold. The old fountain outside my window was covered in a deep layer of white snow, with only parts of the rocks exposed where wind had swept it clean.

I bundled up in my warmest coat and boots with the intention of walking over to Steve's house, my friend who had tried to help me with the ghost. I wanted to tell him all the news of recent happenings, about the secret room and the continued haunting. I only saw him at school on occasion since he was only a junior. Our few brief visits were sporadic.

If I could have crossed over the small creek between our houses, it would have been much faster, but I had to walk all the way around to the bridge and then back to his house. There were Christmas lights shining on some businesses and homes. We only had two more days of school and then would be out on vacation for the holiday.

I wish my heart could have been filled with happiness and the spirit of Christmas, but it wasn't. Holidays were difficult in our home and I'd learned to tether my enthusiasm and expectations. Even though my mom made a big deal out of it – decorated lavishly, cooked scrumptious meals – there was always the undercurrent of fear and anxiety that colored the festive atmosphere.

By the time I reached Steve's house, I was almost frozen from the cold air, but it was also an exhilarating experience. The hills around the valley reflected the light from below and glowed silver, as if we sat in a bowl of fairy dust. The frost sparkled all around on nearby trees and bushes, while the ground was white with a layer of shiny new snow.

I knocked on the door and waited for someone to answer. I had only stood in his yard once before as we visited from the sidewalk. He was usually the one who came to see me. This was the first time I'd gone to his house and knocked on the door.

When a nice lady opened the screen, I asked, "Is Steve home?"

"No, honey, he's not here. He left yesterday on a skiing trip to Sun Valley with his cousins. Was it important? He won't be back until just before Christmas."

"No, I just wanted to visit. Thank you."

Rejected, I walked all the way back home, feeling lonely in the icy winter wonderland. It was dark by the time I got to my room. I turned on the space heater to warm up and listened to the radio for a while. This time, there were more opinions about the latest Free Speech Movement incident where another eight-hundred students were arrested for protesting what many thought was justified civil disobedience. I turned off the radio, grabbed my diary, and began to write about all the new things that had happened today.

After I read a book for some time, I felt tired. Looking at the clock, I saw that there was over an hour before the first visit at eleven. Latching my door, I stood behind the dressing screen and got ready for bed. The door didn't close properly anymore, and there was a space about an inch or so that peeked from the other room. I stared at it and wondered if the ghost peeked through when it stood out there. I suspected that it could walk through the wall if it wanted and move things around, as I had learned the other night when the footstool moved. I still pushed the heavy chair up against the door and attached the string securely over the nail.

With these thoughts swirling in my head, I crawled into bed. The long walk in the winter cold had tired me, and I fell fast asleep, waking only twice during the night at 11 p.m. and at 1 a.m., each time shivering in my bed with fear and unable to move a muscle to investigate when the heavy footsteps thundered through on the other side of my door.

***

Christmas was almost over. I managed to stay out of my room a few nights and avoid the ghost's routine. What with visits from relatives that kept us up late, and a night or two staying elsewhere, our holiday passed quickly. Both Tyke and I agreed it was too cold to work in the cellar chipping away the cement. It would have to wait until warmer weather.

The only real worry I had was the usual fighting between my parents. That consisted of my dad coming home in a bad mood and taking it out on us. Mom did her best to avoid his anger while protecting us, but it seemed to be hopeless as his rage was relentless.

Dad worked hard to provide for our family and so did mom. She was an entertainer and played lovely music on the piano. Working jobs that gradually boosted her career into a popular and profitable occupation, people adored her and her music. I think dad was jealous of that. The many arguments often centered on his accusations against her for imagined misdeeds. She – patiently, but fearfully – endured it all. She never shared her dilemma with us, but we saw and heard it all while we were growing up. She didn't like to talk to us about him and usually distracted us until we were thinking of other things.

We three girls grew up watching this drama – sometimes a life-threatening scene – play out before us. One scene in particular was burned into my memory.

I was five years old and was huddled in bed with my two sisters late at night after we were wakened by my dad yelling at mom in the hallway. She was begging him to be quiet so that we wouldn't be startled awake. In response, he dragged her to our bedroom, flung open the door and flipped on the light. Bright light flooded the room and our eyes opened wide. Mom's face was bloody and the front of dad's white shirt was covered with blood. He said, "You kids awake? Here – look at your mom!"

She reached her hand up to the light switch to turn it off as she attempted to push him from the room, and left a long streak of blood on the wall. He dragged her out and slammed the door leaving the three of us terrified as we clung to each other.

When we woke the next morning, she was unconscious. Our neighbor, Mrs. Jensen had heard the fight the night before and came over as soon as dad left for work. After taking us girls to her house and leaving us there, she took mom to the hospital where she was diagnosed with a broken clavicle, a fractured skull and concussion, broken nose, cracked ribs and numerous contusions (a skiing accident, Mom told the doctor).

In those days, not many people called the police when a husband hit his wife. Mrs. Jensen wanted to call, but my mom wouldn't let her. Mom didn't want anyone to know, especially her family. My dad had threatened her so many times with the murder-suicide that would happen if she ever told – the harm he could do to her parents, his threats against us children accompanied by guns held against our heads – so she kept quiet – to protect her family. There was only one time she turned to her parents for help. They reminded her that, *"she'd made her bed..."* Raised in a strict religious family where weakness was not tolerated, she never asked for help again.

After she came home from the hospital having survived the brutal beating, the first thing she did was to dress us children in nice clothes. Removing all visible bandages, she also dressed up and applied heavy make-up to cover the black bruises. We went to my dad's place of employment where she made sure everyone there saw that we were a happy family, especially *her* – a loving wife, adoring children, content and secure. She squelched any rumors or gossip, so that he could continue to work there as a happy man, and especially to know that he was forgiven and loved by his family.

I was seventeen, now, and still watched his anger build, day after day, until life became intolerable while waiting for the real explosion of emotion that we knew would soon come.

***

Cheryl came out to my room early one cold winter evening. She said she only had a minute because her husband was expected home at any time. Nervously, she added, "I heard from Don today."

I noticed that she frowned and looked at her hands. I thought when people got married, that they were terribly in love and never thought of anyone else again. But watching her, I could see that she was disturbed talking about Don.

"He said he talked to the guys at ISU and they want to come out here and do a ghost investigation."

Suddenly excited, I jumped up and said, "That's great! When?"

"He said in about a month. First, they want to look into the property history as much as possible and then come out. One thing they did find out was that there was a man who lived here, raised vegetables and died in a suspicious fire."

"They found that out? That's what our neighbor said."

"That's one reason why they want to come out."

"Okay, we can do that! We have to keep it a secret, though."

She hesitated for a moment, "He said they need the owners' permission before they can come."

My heart sank. I knew my dad would never give that permission. I felt the tears well in my eyes and turned away, hoping she never saw how disappointed I was. "We both know he won't do that."

Cheryl said, "We could ask him. We could try."

I mumbled, "You know what kind of mood he's in right now? This isn't a good time."

"I know. We could wait a few weeks."

Resigned to forgoing the help of the only people who could solve my problem, I answered, "Yes, maybe we could do that."

She sensed my disappointment and offered, "Look, we're going to the movies tonight. Do you want to come with us?"

Being a third wheel didn't sound that exciting.

She cajoled, "It's a surfing show, double feature."

Feeling a sense of relief, I accepted, "I'd love to go! Sure you don't mind?"

"Not at all; it will get you out of here for a while."

"It sure will." I glanced at the clock, estimating how long we'd be gone. "We won't get home till way after midnight."

She smiled at me with a twinkle in her eye, "Maybe later if we stop for ice cream."

***

We arrived home at 1:15 in the morning, and Cheryl came into the house with me. She had left her scarf at the house earlier and wanted to pick it up. Her husband went on to their apartment.

We were surprised when my dad met us at the front door. He was holding his rifle, his face was red, his hair disheveled and he was mad. Both my sister and I froze at the look on his face.

“Where have you been?” He yelled at me.

“I told you – I went with Cheryl to the movies.”

“I know that’s what you said, but is it what you did? Have you been here all the time or did you come back early? I mean, have you been in your room?”

Confused and scared, I stammered, “N-No, we just got here. I haven’t been out there yet.” I moved over to sit on the couch because my legs were unsteady. Cheryl followed and we sat beside each other.

He began to pace back and forth in front of us, the gun held at his side. “There was someone out in your room.” He angrily strode back and forth, “I heard someone in there – walking around. I grabbed my gun and went out there, expecting to find one of your boyfriends in there with you.”

“I don’t have boyfriends in there – you know that!”

His voice was taut with rage, “I don’t know that – *when I hear what I heard; s*omeone walking around *in your room*!*”*

I looked up, the expression on my face one of astonishment. When I found my voice, I asked, “What time?”

Irritated, he looked at his watch, “About fifteen minutes ago. I went out there,” he lifted his gun, to let me know he had been ready to shoot someone. “But you were gone. You were out there weren't you, hiding somewhere?" he accused, his eyes bright with anger.

Resignation sounded strongly in my shaking voice when I bowed my head and answered, "I told you – there's a ghost out there!"

He stopped pacing and leaned down into my face, "You expect me to believe that?"

I began to cry, scared at his anger, scared of the gun, not knowing what to do or what to say.

He yelled, "I heard loud footsteps! Not some ghost!" He began to pace again, still holding the gun. His voice was low and controlled when he said, "I'm gonna tell you this only *one more time* – I better not find out that you are letting anyone into your room!"

I sobbed as I explained, "I hear the footsteps every night! They come at a certain time! I don't know who it is, I've tried to find out but none of my friends are doing it. No one that I know is doing it!" I buried my head against the couch.

He stopped yelling, but I knew he didn't believe me. Before he turned to go back to his bedroom, he ordered, "I don't believe *any* of your bull – ! You stay in here tonight."

Cheryl was shaking when she leaned close to me and whispered, "Come on, you can sleep in my old room. I don't think you want to stay in there, but you might have to."

Wiping tears from my cheeks, I said, "I don't want to, I love my room, but it's so awful out there. I don't know what to do!"

"Don't cry, you'll think of something. At least one good thing came from all this."

Dumbfounded, I asked, "What?"

"He heard the ghost, too."

The color drained from my face, "Yes, he did, but he said the footsteps came *from my room*! That's the only way he could have heard them. The ghost was in there walking around because I was gone!"

The ghost was reclaiming its space, as if it was resolute to own the room, and was determined to drive me out!

Possession

"He hides in the shadows, invisible and terrifying..."

Revised diary entries January... 1965

Christmas was finally over, but my dad was still mad. I avoided him as much as possible because if I came within his range in any way, he zeroed in on me. I couldn't seem to do anything right, as if I was now the enemy.

His bad mood affected the whole family, and my mom tried to buffer us children. She was a happy person who saw the good in everyone. No one tried harder in her marriage then she did. She knew my dad had shortcomings but always said he was a very smart man. She reminded us about what happened to him in the war – his almost fatal injury when his comrade found him, and instead of helping, he riffled through his pockets, stealing all his valuables. He then left my dad for dead – only dad hadn't died. At that time, he'd been conscious enough to recognize his robber.

After he returned home and the war ended, he searched for that guy. All he would ever say about it was, "He'll never rob anyone again."

I always wondered what that meant.

When I questioned my mom as to why she would stay married to him, her answer was simple. She said she loved him. In spite of his flaws, she wanted to stay by his side. Whether out of fear or devotion, I always wondered.

Years ago, he had agreed to see a doctor concerning his "nerves". After the diagnosis that meant years of psychological therapy and drug treatment, he refused to go back, claiming that the doctor was mistaken and there was nothing wrong with him.

The new month of January was hazy in my memory. Even my diary entries are short and somewhat emotional. A new year was upon us, but the old problems were still very much part of our lives.

My tensions had almost reached a breaking point as the pressure of the hauntings was becoming more tangible. The presence of the apparition permeated the air in my room. It felt heavy, thick and oppressive. Whatever happiness I'd enjoyed there seemed to disappear, consumed by the palpable manifestation that continued to occur on a daily basis. My senses were beginning to blur and concentration was more difficult.

***

"Dear Diary,

I feel like I'm in a dark place right now. On the surface, I'm just a normal teen, getting good grades, enjoying friendships with great friends, dating and attending what I'm supposed to attend. But inside, hidden under all the pretense, is the real story; the constant worry about my parents, the fear of my dad, the frustration of unsuccessfully dealing with the ghost problem, and just an overall depression that settles over me. When I'm alone and not pretending, I see all the failure and feel the frustration. One of the things that once brightened my day was the happiness I felt in my very own room. Now, that is gone. Am I losing control over my mind? Is the influence of the ghost seeping into my soul? I wonder if the thoughts that it felt when alive are becoming my thoughts."

There is no cold like January cold. The little space heater in my room worked hard to generate any heat. I finished my homework that evening and then cuddled on the bed wrapped in a warm blanket.

Outside, the moon danced high in a clear sky, lighting away the stars as moonlight reflected off the snow covered earth that sparkled like scattered diamonds. Approaching black clouds sat hunched near the distant hills, crouching low and slowly creeping closer as stealthy as a panther.

That evening, I moved the bed around in my room. My sister Tyke helped me.

"I liked it the old way," she said as she scrutinized the arrangement.

"Sometimes, change is good," I theorized.

As she plumped up the pillows, she kept looking around before she said, "Do you want me to stay with you tonight?"

"What? You said you would never stay out here!"

"Well, I can change my mind can't I?"

I jumped up, so happy that she would stay with me at last! "What changed your mind?"

She looked down and her cheeks flushed. "Dad wanted to take some pictures again."

My stomach twisted as the memory of that ritual flooded my mind. As little girls, we thought it was what we were supposed to do – pose provocative, etc. We were older now and knew better. Tyke, being the youngest, especially felt the pressure and the wrath when she refused. He terrified her.

I took a moment to breath, "Did he touch you?"

She quickly answered, “No. I got away from him. Then mom came home.”

I felt tears prick at my eyes as I fought off the memories of his abuse. I mumbled, “I wish he’d fallen down into the old well and died.”

“Me, too.”

I swallowed my tears and said, “It would have been a blessing.”

Tyke leaned against me with her arms crossed around herself as if she was ashamed of her young girl body. That was how we all felt about ourselves, how he made us feel, because of how he looked at us, how he touched us, and the things he did to us.

“Don’t go back in the house,” I cautioned.

“He left with mom. They have to play for a party tonight and won’t be home until after midnight.”

“Did she know what he wanted to do with you?”

“I think so.”

We didn’t say anything else because we’d been through this before, many times. Mom did her best to protect us, and she paid a heavy price. We had to watch out for each other whenever she was gone.

***

"Dear Diary,

...I still can't believe that Cheryl got married. She is so lucky to get away from home. I know she'll be happy. Her life here hasn't been a very happy one. There was always dad to worry about; she was just a little girl when mom married him. Even then, he did things to her that was wrong. Mom told us to never tell anyone and we haven't. His threats to kill us force us to keep his secrets. We just try to look out for each other as much as we can.

Once, when I was about ten years old, mom was in the hospital. Tyke was over at gramma's house and I was supposed to watch out for Cheryl if dad came home. She was thirteen years old and such a pretty girl. He didn't care that I was there. He grabbed her while she cried. He laughed and pretended to be tickling her and she wrapped her arms around herself and tried to not let him see her tears. He would be mad about that. His hands were all over her body. I tried to pull them apart and get between them but he threw me across the room. Then he pushed her onto the bed. In a panic, I ran out of the house and down the middle of the road, sobbing and crying for help! It was secluded where we lived and no one heard me.

By some miracle, mom was coming home. She was driving down the road because she had left the hospital before she was supposed to. She picked me up.

I don't remember what happened after that. Lots of memories are blocked from my mind and that's probably a good thing..."

***

Tyke said, "I need to get my clothes. I'll be right back."

I looked outside to make sure his car was gone. "Do you want me to come with you?"

"No. He's gone and it will only take me a few minutes."

While she was gone, I kept the radio on and sorted through my books. At school, there were lists of suggested reading matter for my age group. I wanted to read all the books listed, and so I read a variety of subjects. One book, The Carpetbaggers, a popular book at that time and *on the list*, had surprised me. I stopped reading it at a certain point because it was, in my opinion, not worthy of my time.

I heard the door open and my sister ran inside, looking behind her at the shadows. I could tell she was trying to be brave.

For a while, we talked and laughed and were silly. After that, we played some board games until we were bored with them. I picked up my book.

Tyke was sitting cross-legged on the bed, her robe wrapped around her legs. She was flipping through old '45's looking for a certain song. "I should go get my record player and we could listen to some good music."

"It's getting late," I answered.

After I changed into nightclothes, I checked the door to make sure the string was hooked over the nail. Then I pushed the heavy chair up against it. "There, that should hold the door in place."

The music on the radio was replaced with current news and reaching over, I turned it off. The only sound now was the hum of the motor in the heater.

Tyke yawned and crawled under the covers. “I hope I can sleep tonight. It’s spooky out here.”

I could tell she was sleepy. “Don’t worry; we can protect each other if anything happens. I’m so happy you are here.”

I wasn’t ready to sleep yet because I had a lot on my mind. I reached for my book but my thoughts wandered.

A new semester had started at school, the beginning of the last semester of my senior year. Soon it would be graduation time. These thoughts interrupted my reading and I turned back a few pages to begin again, since I couldn’t remember what I’d just read. I finally closed the book and yawned.

I stood up and observed my clean room. Some changes felt good and reorganizing the desk and shelves was refreshing. My headboard now rested against the same wall as the door. Before, it was across the room and when I lay in bed, I faced the door. It was always disturbing to stare at the door – watching for movement.

Since I moved it the other way around, now when I lay in bed, I stared at the other wall that was decorated with photos and other memorabilia. The only way I could see the door was to turn onto my side in bed facing the doorway. Then it was only a few feet away from my face.

The new arrangement was pleasing. I turned off the heater and light then settled into bed. I knew the clock was marching on and that it would soon be time.

Tyke yawned again and snuggled down deep into the blankets.

I asked her, “Do you remember when we lived in Montana and how cold it got at night?”

"You mean that old shack Dad made us live in, no heat and forty degrees below zero? Yes, I remember."

I remembered too. "The only way we could sleep at night was to sandwich ourselves together. I kept your back warm for a while and then we'd turn over and it was your turn to warm mine."

She shivered, "I'll never forget how cold we were."

I added, "Mom would put sealed jugs filled with boiling water at our feet but by morning, they would be frozen solid ice."

"Was that when you were sick with Tuberculosis?"

"Yes."

Cold air, blood-splattered coughing, and devastating illness mixed into the memories.

The bright moonlight shown through the window, and cast shadows across the furniture when I recalled, "A glowing lady dressed in white sat by our bed at night…an angel."

I watched the play of light until it slowly began to dim as the dark clouds in the distance stole across the moonlight and gentled its glow. I listened as my sisters soft breath became even and steady. She was asleep.

The quiet was peaceful and having Tyke staying the night was reassuring and comforting. My thoughts settled into softer subjects, happier times and soothing memories. The night would soon pass and the sun would surely come up again.

The reflective moment was suddenly gone when I heard the outside door open, the window rattle loudly before it slammed shut. Then the footsteps marched noisily up to my door.

My heart pounded louder and the rising fear began to grow in my chest. I glanced at Tyke who still slept deeply. Lying in bed,

I turned on my side and stared at the door that wouldn't shut anymore. In fact, that morning, I discovered that the last hinge had given way and nothing held the door in place any longer. I leaned it up against the doorway frame, jostled it a bit to make sure it was firm, before I latched the string and pushed the heavy chair against it. The only problem was the gap that appeared along the side of the door – where it leaned against the frame. It was a solid door and wouldn't move easily, but from my position in bed, the dark gap extended down the side and was open to my inspection, beckoning like a peephole.

I closed my eyes, afraid of what I might see and waited for the ghost to leave. That had been its new habit – silently waiting a few minutes before leaving the same way it had come. I listened for heavy breathing, opening my eyes for a second and registering for the first time how close I was to the gap in the door. It would be easy to hear breathing from this distance.

The dim glow of silver moonlight colored the furniture and climbed up the walls before darkness covered the light. Still, there was no sound from the other side.

I couldn't stop staring at the gap, trying to see movement, or even the white vapor of human breath that sometimes steamed in cold weather. I saw nothing except blackness. I heard nothing except complete stillness, always shocking after the noise and commotion the ghost made whenever it entered.

The time ticked on as I held my own breath, waiting for it to leave, waiting to hear any tiny sound – a scrape of a boot, a whisper of movement, or the sure sound when it might turn to leave. I was so close to the door and was sure I could hear that.

As I waited, the passing of time seemed forever, and since I was afraid to move to look at the time, I could only speculate how much had passed. My eyes were getting weary and I told myself that maybe the ghost had changed its routine again and had reverted to its original haunting. Back to the beginning of the hauntings when it would walk in but never leave.

It was almost a comforting thought at that moment as more time passed while I stared at the dark gap in the doorway, waiting for what would happen next. Maybe nothing would happen next.

Maybe –

As if in slow motion, my eyes glued to the edge of the door, watching the view into the other side, the door started to move. It slowly moved forward, falling back into my room – falling as if pushed from the top – hitting and rolling over the heavy chair and continuing to fall over the chair until it hit the floor on the other side. The door hit hard and bounced sideways, crashing into the wall and rocking back and forth, as it lay haphazard across the footstool, the loud noise shattering the stillness.

I cannot describe the terror that rose inside me to see the barrier broken down – *pushed*, not unbalanced, but *pushed* from the direction of the other room! It took a lot of strength to do that to a solid hard wood door and make it flip right over the top of the heavy chair until it crashed against the wall!

I sat up in bed as the wispy moonlight colored the scene in ghostly white, mottled gray, and pitch black.

Suddenly, my sister grabbed me. I'd almost forgotten she was there. Holding her hand across her mouth, her eyes bulging, she whispered, "I saw that! What happened?"

"Shhhhh…"

My body felt frozen in place, a soft silent breath was the only sound as the air escaped my mouth. I waited…

Slowly, I scooted as far from the dark open doorway as I could in my bed, clear to the other side near my sister, while I waited for the ghost to enter the room. There was no doubt in my mind that it was there and had taken possession of this room. As if the ghost stood there in all its indiscernible might and strength, emanating evil, I felt the presence and cowered.

At last, I would meet my tormentor, the invisible, unknown threat that now dwelled within the only space that I had dared call my own.

I couldn't move a muscle and slid down into the bed, the covers held against my neck. I felt dizzy when I realized I wasn't breathing. In fact, I wondered if I could pass out from fear. I'd heard the phrase, "scared silly", and now I knew what it meant. In my mind, I kept seeing the door slowly roll over the heavy chair and crash down, making a loud sound shattering the silence of the moonlight. The terror renewed inside me each time I envisioned it over and over in my mind as it played like a broken record.

I could feel my sister shivering beside me and I held her hand tightly. She shouldn't be here; this wasn't her fault. I was the one who had intruded the ghost's sanctuary. I was the one who challenged for its home.

I waited for the entity to enter, waited for it to leave, hoping to hear the footsteps, the outside door open, the window rattle in its frame – but I heard nothing. No sound whatsoever came from the dark space. I knew the ghost was right where it wanted to be, back in its place.

When I had first moved into my cherished bedroom, the entity wasn't strong enough to drive me out, but over the past months, the specter had found strength. Whatever fed its growth or increased its determination and gave it life – had succeeded. It was here.

I had been a fool to think I could own this room.

Afraid to make a sound, afraid to even whisper quietly, we lay side by side and watched the night until it passed. It was a long eerie night that resembled one continuous nightmare. I don't think I even blinked as the hours ticked by until daylight began to brighten the space.

When the light crept inside, we sat up. In shock, we crawled out of bed, slipped on our shoes and ran from the room.

Flight

"The hush of ghostly sound..."

I was spending more time in the house, sleeping there at night, but was drawn to my room. I wasn't looking for solitude or comfort – not anymore. I viewed my room as a dying dream. Looking at the pretty furniture and decorated walls, I could understand why it had once been shut away, closed off and forgotten. No matter how pretty it was painted or furnished, or filled with dreams – it was doomed. No matter how hard I had tried, my efforts to bring new life and happiness to those four walls were crushed. Something else was stronger than I was – stronger than any other inhabitants had been – for many years. When the noise in the night – the footsteps, the slamming door – had not scared me away, the ghost changed tactics. As its strength grew, the entity was empowered to do more.

The heaviness and oppressiveness of its essence brought my spirit down until I keenly felt the depression. My pretty bed with the quilted headboard, the light pink dresser, the treasured bookshelf now stood alone. I could not bring love and warmth to the room. It may as well have been empty again, locked up, barricaded, and shut away from human tenancy.

On the day after the door was pushed down, I took my sister with me when I was finally brave enough to go back in there.

The day was cold and gray, locked in winter's grip. There was the door, still lying across the footstool against the wall, the heavy chair unmoved from its place. The atmosphere was changed. No longer a sunny room with dreams of happiness enfolded within, it felt of sadness and ancient grudges. The silence was charged with despair.

I gathered what I needed and left the cold depressed room. I knew that if I stayed in that room, it would destroy me. The physical sickness that assaulted me whenever I thought of staying out there again drove me back into the house where I slept in Cheryl's old room, now converted into Mom's treasure room, or shared my little sister's small room, night after night.

The memory of the falling door would haunt me for years, invade my dreams, and sometimes startle me awake. I had to accept that I had lost the fight. My hopes that the ghost hunters from ISU could help were abandoned because my dad would never let them come.

***

Sometime at the end of the month, another day began. I woke up to get ready for school. I was staying in Tyke's room again. The night before, we had been awakened by the commotion of my parents fighting. My dad was yelling at mom, and she was trying to persuade him to be quiet, her voice soft and low. After they moved into their bedroom, we couldn't hear anything more, so we went back to sleep.

Mom was usually in the kitchen preparing breakfast before we went to school, but that morning she wasn't. Dad had left for work early before we were awake. Looking for her, I knocked on her bedroom door and went in. The room was dark and she was curled up in bed. I called out and she turned over, shielding her face with her hand. Her voice was unrecognizable when she spoke.

I was horrified to find her semi-conscious, her face badly beaten, swollen, black and blue. The bedding was covered in blood. I didn't have to ask her who did this because I already knew. She could barely talk because of her swollen mouth and couldn't move because of broken ribs.

My stomach twisted as fear and revulsion squeezed inside me. I knew it had gone too far. She was too old to take a beating as bad as this one was. Maybe she could endure this in her younger years, but by now, she deserved to live without a beating. She deserved a peaceful life.

I was sick and angry. He had done this to her and then left to go to work. I couldn't bear to live here any longer and be a witness to this senseless abuse, especially to someone so dear to me as my mother. I sat beside her on the bed and gently brushed my hand along her arm.

She tried to apologize – for not being up to see us off to school – for not making our breakfast. Between words, she would pass out and then come-to again, continuing with her slurred words of regrets.

Tyke came into the room. She whispered, "What happened? Is she all right?"

"No, he hurt her again." When I turned to face her, I saw that she had tears in her eyes. I blinked mine back and stood up.

Taking her arm, I led her out of the room. "We can't stay here any longer."

"What can we do? Where can we go? He'll just find us and then you know what will happen…"

I shook my head, feeling as perplexed as she was. It made me angry that we were here in this house, and always frightened of him and what he might do. In fact, we'd lived our whole lives like that.

I also knew that if we left, it could be a death sentence for all of us. He would keep his threats and promises of the past; the threat to find us if we ever left and the promise to kill us.

Looking around I said, "I don't want to leave – my friends – school, and everything, but we have to do something! He'll kill her someday!"

Tyke whispered, "She's too hurt to go. He'll kill us if we leave."

"She's too hurt to stay! He'll expect dinner on the table tonight when he comes home! What then? Even if we take care of it and he finds her in bed, you know what he'll do." I thought of all the years of abuse – our tears when he would grab us and pull us onto his lap – our futile efforts to escape.

I knew right then that I had to make a choice, no matter how difficult it would be.

Tyke said, "Whatever you want to do, I'll help."

My sister and I formed a plan. We packed as much of our stuff as we could fit into the car. Then we carefully wrapped mom in blankets and helped her to the car, laying her gently on the back seat supported by pillows. She could barely walk, stumbling many times, and mostly unaware of what was going on. I told her we were leaving. She resisted, begging in her half-conscious way, her words slurred, to stay, afraid of what he would do if we left.

I checked myself out of school and then my sister. She was crying to have to leave her friends. We sold what we could at a pawnshop to get some money. I knew I could never call the police or take that route, so Tyke and I drove away, with our very hurt, sick mom in the back seat.

That's what we did, that morning, that very day.

We went as far away as we could.

When we stopped, we took mom to a doctor, and it took a few weeks for her to recover. We found a place to live and I checked myself into a new high school, also putting Tyke into school. We told no one where we were, afraid my dad would come after us and hurt us. We told Cheryl we were leaving, but not where we were going.

That was a secret we never shared.

Ashes

"A door closes but...?"

I left behind the haunted room and the ghost who continued to lurk in the shadows of the Fountain Courts. The hidden room in the cellar that was only partially revealed kept its secrets as it had done for so many years. Whatever was almost exposed behind that cement wall, was once again, forgotten.

Not only did I lose my beloved bedroom, but also we had to leave all our friends in the middle of a school year and start again in a new school and new town.

In the end, it was a small sacrifice for our freedom.

The memory of my beautiful room had been corroded by the evil influence of a ghost, a spirit who still owned the space and refused to let go.

Time passed, and mom slowly healed. I finished school, graduated that spring, and started collage the next year. My sister and I waited over a year before we returned for a visit. We missed our friends, our old hangouts, and even the old neighborhood. We were only able to do this because my dad no longer cared about mom or us. He'd found a younger woman with a few small children who moved in with him. We all felt sorry for her.

I wondered about the ghost. The haunted footsteps continued to echo, as my dad reported hearing a trespasser in that room.

On our visit, I went out to look at my old room. It stood empty, with only the bedframe left, the lovely pearl-quilted satin headboard, stained and dirty. A sad room held captive by an entity who demanded possession. I walked around, listening to the echo of my footsteps, and remembered the other footsteps that haunted me even now.

Tyke came in and we stood in the middle of the dusty floor where my bed once stood. She commented, "It looks a lot bigger with all your stuff gone."

I rubbed my hands up my arms, feeling the goosebumps that prickled. "I know." I stepped to the window and peeked out. The fountain was full of weeds where a ring of water would have been when the fountains worked. Mom planted petunias around that circle when she was here that would cascade down the edge in a colorful waterfall. When she left this place, the weeds had returned.

"It's not my room anymore, that's for sure." I didn't know what else to say. I had lost so much and the room that once promised happiness was now an empty shell of shattered dreams.

Glancing into the closet, I saw something on the high shelf above the thick wooden dowel that once held my clothes. Reaching up, I grabbed hold of a book, left behind.

Brushing off the dust, I moved closer to the window so that I could read the cover: *The Haunting of Hill House.*

As if it burned my fingers, I tossed it on the floor. I remembered that I'd been reading that book when I first heard the ghost. I had never finished reading it after that night.

The book landed with its pages open. Bending down I picked it up again and read the open page. The words seemed to jump out at me.

"Within, walls continued upright, bricks met neatly, floors were firm, and doors were sensibly shut; silence lay steadily against the wood and stone of Hill House, and whatever walked there, walked alone."

I slowly closed the pages and laid the book back on the floor.

Tyke said, "Let's go."

We left the Fountain Courts and never returned while it was still standing. I could almost feel the haunted eyes of the ghost watching me from the dark corners of the room as I walked away. It would stay forever, but I had to leave.

***

"Dear Diary,

...Today I went back to my old room. I dreaded what was there but I had to see it one more time. It's hard to go back because so much has changed. Who wants to go back to such terrible memories? I know the ghost is still there and I feel sorry for it, hanging on to something that was only a dream that has ended. It should let go and move on. That's what I had to do, what I was forced to do. Even though it was difficult, it was for the better..."

***

Eventually, my dad remodeled the old apartment number fifteen to rent out, but no one would stay there for long and it usually stood vacant. I know exactly what went on in that room and the impossibility of someone being able to live there.

As the years passed, I often thought of my experience, and still puzzled about the ghost and why it haunted. Eventually, my busy life would bring me back to Pocatello some twenty years later in about 1988. It really wasn't my choice to return. My mother was ill and since she had moved back into the city, I felt I needed to be near her. My dad was dead by then, and the old place belonged to someone else. I was told that he died in that house, alone in the night, inside his bedroom, just on the other side of the wall from my old room where the ghost walked.

Twenty-plus-years had changed the city and much of it was new to me. I still remembered the old house, my memories of the haunting still clear in my mind.

I refused to go anywhere near the old Fountain Courts as those memories always haunted me. I shared some of the story with my children, but not the depth of the fear and anxiety I had felt. There was more to the story than I could ever tell them.

In 1996, two of my older sons decided to go back to the haunted apartment of the old Fountain Courts. Without telling me, they went in the dark of the night.

Their plan unknown to the current owner, they found my old apartment and went into the cellar. The floor was littered with debris and was oddly scattered with old-fashioned toys that were rusted and strewn about. They discovered that the wall hiding the secret room still stood and the hole that we'd labored so hard to make, was mended with cement. The old well was covered with a piece of plywood. The boys shoved it aside and peeked into the deep, dark well, still open and unsecure.

The apartment above stood empty, but was locked so they could only peek into the windows. The two old fountains still stood in front, their solid rock exterior little changed, as they continued their sentinel. The complex was run down and no longer cared for, as the years seemed to consume it.

Sometime shortly after the new twenty-first century began, the entire place burned to the ground. Even in its decayed state, it was considered a landmark location in Pocatello and many lamented its loss. Since the old apartments were in such decline, there could have been many reasons it caught fire. I believed that it was the malice of the ghost – to burn down the place in the same manner as his old house had been burned so many years ago. I wondered if this satisfied its compulsion to linger and if the ghost was able to move on.

I finally returned to Fountain Courts one more time – to see it in ruins, burned to the ground and sunken into its cellar. It was quite a sight. The big old trees still stood, even though they were old and showing signs of deterioration. The two old fountains made of river rock still stood strong, their sides blackened by fire; as if they wanted to remind of days gone by, days when the old place was once beautiful and had meaning – maybe a reminder to me of what I learned when I lived there about tragedy, endurance, and renewal.

Someone rebuilt a new apartment complex in the same spot. It is more modern and completely different from the old Fountain Courts.

Even now, one thing that is still the same, the two stately fountains, at least a hundred years old, still stand sentinel and watch over the old grounds that once belonged to a simple vegetable farmer who disappeared, but never really left or surrendered his property. If he was the ghost who haunted – and I believe he was – then his story is yet to be told; not the one after his death, but the story before that – the story of what really happened to him and why he lingered behind for so long. He was forced to give up his life when he was alive, but no one could force him to abandon his home even after death. I know because I tried. No one tried harder than I, but his will was stronger than mine.

Some things have stayed in my mind even after many years have passed. I can't forget the terror I felt or the way it paralyzed me so that I was unable to act rationally. I learned that I was afraid of the unknown. I still am.

The most terrifying night of my life was when I witnessed the ghost's great strength – *physical* strength, when the entity pushed over the heavy door, that dark night so long ago. If it could do that, what else could it do? I think that door weighed more than I did, and if the specter could push it halfway across the room and into the wall, it could do the same to me. That was when I gave up.

Last entry – 1965

"Dear Diary,

I'm so sad. We had to leave – my friends, my school, my life. We had to protect mom and take her far away. This will be the last time I write my thoughts here or share my dreams. Just because I wish it to come true, doesn't mean it will. You have been my wish diary, my dream diary, my hopeful diary. Now I have to face the truth of life and choose a direction. I choose to do what will protect and help my mom and sister. It doesn't matter what I wanted in the past. I just want us to be safe from dad forever..."

***

I tucked the diary away, deep into a box, where it lay for many years, forgotten and unread. It was really a story about a ghost who drove me away; a ghost who forced me to let go of youthful dreams and to face reality. The ghost of Fountain Courts wasn't able to move past tragedy or to forgive what life had done. The ghost couldn't let go.

I guess it didn't want much – only its small space of earth and to be left alone to walk at night, slamming the door, the footsteps heavy in an empty room…

Alone…

Linda and Tyke in front of fountain 1966

The two old fountains, over 100 years old, still stand in Pocatello, Idaho in 2019 (2nd fountain is in far back of pic) They can be viewed from the Portneuf Greenway walking trail at the southern end of W. Carter St.

About the author: Linda Gatewood

Writing was a hobby for Linda Gatewood while she raised her seven children. Occasionally authoring a few newspaper articles and stories, she has written mainly for pure enjoyment and satisfaction. She previously published the *Winter Secret series*, a romantic suspense that consists of four books, ***Winter Secret, Spring Promise, Summer Truth*** ***and Autumn Hush***. ***A Chance to Remember*** followed. Co-authoring an historical nonfiction with her son, Aaron Werner, was a step into a new genre. ***The Legend of Clevengers Lost Gold*** was a thrill to work on.

Ms. Gatewood lives in the beautiful state of Idaho.

Please turn this page

for a preview of

Linda Gatewood's

New romantic suspense novel,

Timely Rendezvous

Available soon on Amazon.com

Away

When Anna first visited her new rental, she went at night. The sky above glimmered bright with midnight starlight while the moon drifted slowly behind waves of clouds. The heavy air enclosed the silence that ensured her desire for secrecy. All the details of the contract for the house had been handled over the internet, her anonymity vital in the transaction. The name she used would suffice for now since her real name, Anna Gibson, had been kept secret. She had no choice.

The small house was located far from any other inhabitants. The trail in front ended at a dead end a few feet from the building. According to the advertisement, this secluded cabin was only used for recreational fishermen who dared to float down the great Salmon River in the wilderness of central Idaho. Anna turned the flashlight on the front door before she put the key into the lock.

The journey here had been frightening. She had never traveled so far into such isolation before and the experience left her feeling shaky and nervous. Her car was a mile away in a covered car shelter. She had to follow a trail from there, pulling her luggage behind her in the dark. This wasn't exactly where she wanted to be right now, but circumstances had placed her here. Everything had changed now. Her instincts had led her thus far, along with highly inflamed adrenalin for self-preservation. She had handled the situation with control, but it never changed who she really was. The bone-shaking fear she carried inside was still there and growing every day.

When a great horned owl sailed out across the pathway, on his way to another forest, she was startled by its silvery shape with wings outstretched, the silent flight unnerving. Ducking under the eve of the cabin, she fumbled and dropped the key held in her hand. Chiding herself, she whispered, “Get a grip, Anna!”

Groping for the key, she knelt down on the steps. The air smelled of pine-scented needles, for they had fallen everywhere. A twig snapped in the dark forest where nature’s inhabitants sheltered safely in the shadows. Anna brushed aside the length of long soft hair that fell forward. In its folds, the bright moon above reflected its deep, honey color.

After retrieving the key, she opened the door and stepped inside. The light switch was nearby and when touched, revealed the living room of her new home. There was a large fireplace against the wall with stacks of split wood nearby, creating a cozy and clean atmosphere.

Anna carried her luggage into the bedroom. The bed had been freshly made up by the rental service and included a token stuffed grizzly teddy bear. She gently set him aside and put her things away before she went into the kitchen. Everything she would need while staying here was available, including dinnerware and a refrigerator stocked with food. It all seemed so perfect. She carefully looked into every corner, making sure no one was hiding there. After the experience she’d had before coming here, her nerves were raw.

She checked her cell phone. As promised, there was service in the house but she had been warned that further down the trail, cell phone service ended. She quickly punched the number of her former roommate, Kimberly.

Slipping off her shoes, she said, “Hi, Kim! Just want to let you know that I made it.”

On the other end of the line, Kim scolded, “I wish you hadn’t done this. It’s just too far away – not only that, I don’t even know where you are! I only know you are somewhere in Idaho – somewhere in the wilderness, far away from Maine!”

“I know, believe me I don’t want to be here.” She subconsciously listened for any noises outside. “My house is lovely, the area is beautiful and best of all, isolated.” She stood up and peeked out the window looking for shadows that moved in the dark. “You know I had no choice.”

Her friend sniffed, tears in her voice, “I hate it that my best friend has to hide. It’s not fair.”

“It won’t be forever.”

“It might be. I still haven’t been able to get ahold of Norman.”

“Not yet?”

“No, and it worries me. He and I are the only ones who know you left.”

Anna’s voice lost confidence as her heart sank. “He must have a good reason.”

“I don’t trust him.”

“Kim, you’ve never liked Norman.”

"No, he gives me the creeps. You don't like him either. He might be your boss, but he's strange."

Anna laughed nervously, "Maybe we misjudged him."

"You always give others the benefit of the doubt! For starters, there's something untrustworthy in him – like he'd sell his grandmother up the river for a dollar!"

Anna smiled, "He's always been fair to me."

"That's because you work endless hours doing his bidding."

"I like my job."

"I never understood your fascination for old stuffy things – especially books!" Kim quickly added, "Scott Taylor called for you."

Anna stiffened, and took a deep breath, "You didn't tell him, did you?"

"No. I did as you asked. He seemed heart-broken. You really did dump him, didn't you?"

"It was over a long time ago." For a moment, she clearly remembered the last time she saw him, the last time her bright, green eyes had sparkled just for him, right before he betrayed her, disappointed her and revealed his true character. Somewhere, deep inside, she should have hurt more – but didn't. Maybe the break-up with Scott had been gradually happening for some time and she was almost prepared. Maybe in her heart, she had already left him. The memory of how Scott hurt her still burned, but it didn't cut like a knife anymore. His betrayal no longer humiliated her, although the dreams that she had shared with him were once again locked up tight inside her – the hope for a future with someone who loved her.

"Thank you, Kim. I'll call again soon."

She laid the phone aside as apprehension washed over her. Her boss, Norman, must have a reason for putting her in such a precarious position. It was baffling, and created doubts about him and his motives.

She noticed a note lying on the small table. Picking it up, she found instructions about the house from the rental agency.

"There is a shed down by the river with a boat and fishing gear. The boat isn't built for floating on the Salmon, just for fishing in the small inlet. If you want a bigger boat, please let us know. We only come out once a week for cleaning and restocking. If you need anything before then, please call our office. Enjoy your vacation."

She set it aside, having no intentions of fishing on the great Salmon River or the gentler inlet. She pulled out her laptop. There were still questions, and the sooner things were settled, the sooner she could go home. She wasn't even sure what to expect, yet, and for the next half hour, her efforts to learn more continued in confusion.

Her cell phone startled her when it rang. She could see that it was Norman calling. As soon as she answered, he began to talk excitedly.

"Anna, did you make it?"

"Yes, I just got here."

He paused before he implored, “Won’t you please tell me where you are?”

“Norman, we already had this conversation. I can’t”

“How can I help you if I don’t know where you are?”

“For starters, you can fix the problem you caused. Then I can come back and not worry about finding a knife in my back.”

“I can’t. Not yet.”

“Why?”

“I don’t have all the answers. You need to tell me where you are so that I can protect you.”

“I can protect myself. After that experience at my apartment, I learned a lesson. Since this has my name all over it, Norman, I’m the one in danger, not you…just me. I’m depending on you to fix this. I came to you for help – not for this. I can’t hide forever.” She waited for a response and could hear his soft breath on the line. She asked, “Is there something you haven’t told me?”

There was no answer, as they were suddenly cut off. Anna stared at her phone wondering if he hung up or if something else interfered. With her heart racing, she stood up and made sure the door was locked and all the windows were secure. Outside, it was pitch black and the only sound was the roar of the distant river as it raged through the steep walls of the canyon. She had to remind herself how careful she’d been. There was no way someone could have followed her. Tomorrow, she would explore her new home, but tonight she was tired, not only physically, but also mentally, as well.

In the bathroom, she turned on the shower. While she waited for the water to warm, she noticed a spray can on the counter with a note attached. "*Please carry this bear spray with you when walking in the woods.*" She shuddered, remembering her mile long trek here on foot without any defense. She closed her green tinted eyes for a moment before she undressed and stepped under the hot water. Her day had been long, tough and filled with tension. Had she covered her tracks? Could someone have managed to follow her? If so, *who was that someone?*

Anna wrapped a towel around her body and crawled into bed. The tension that had plagued her all day began to seep away. The soft comfort of a feathered duvet was warm and protected her while she lay there. She closed her eyes and listened to the sound of gentle breezes that moved the trees above. She soon escaped into soothing rest.

***

The morning dawned with a chill in the air. Summer was drawing to a close, and in this part of the country, autumn came fast. After she dressed, Anna slipped a shawl around her shoulders and approached the fireplace. Her early years as a girl scout would finally come in handy. It wasn't long until she had a cozy fire that warmed with a beautiful scent of pine. She sat near the flame and opened the bag that contained the book.

She lifted the book and held it in her hands. This was where all the trouble began. She ran her fingers across the intricate, leather engraving that was also beautifully colored. The cover alone was a work of art, the book preciously preserved for generations. Anyone could see that it was a treasure without even knowing the contents. The title was prominent across the front, its delicate letters surrounded by scribed vines – *Rendezvous*.

She left her hand on the word as she remembered the first time she saw the book. Her great Aunt Emelia had been confined to a home for the elderly for many years. Anna visited at least once a month since there were no other members of the family left, just her and great Aunt Em. On the last visit, her aunt was poorly. She gave Anna a key to a box and made her promise to guard the contents always.

With a soft voice, her aunt said, “That key will bring joy into your life.” That was the last thing she ever said to Anna.

After the funeral, Anna collected the box. With grave regard for her aunt’s wishes, she waited until she was along in her apartment before she opened it.

She found the book nestled inside. It charmed her from the beginning, beguiling her curiosity. There was something enchanting about its manuscript, as if it was the only copy in the world. It had been created for one particular soul, by one other singular individual. The poems contained inside were written by a similar hand, authored by different people, and all dedicated to a mysterious woman named Abbigail.

Beneath the book and also stored inside the locked box, was an old family album of pictures. It contained photos of her aunt when she was only a child. Anna found pictures of herself as a baby and several of her parents. This was a treasure, indeed.

After further investigation of the book called *Rendezvous*, she became concerned about the possible value of the old manuscript. There was no doubt that it was rare and could be worth a fortune. It was no longer locked up in a box, but sat near her bed in the apartment. Her neighborhood was as safe as any ordinary neighborhood, which didn't speak well of keeping valuables protected.

Anna's Boss, Norman, owned a high-end antique shop, and the next morning she took the book with her to get his opinion. That was her first mistake.

The fire snapped loudly and she jumped.

She lifted her hand from the book, stood up and walked to the window to look outside. The sun was shining through the many branches of pines that surrounded the little house. She remembered that she planned to explore today to become familiar with her surroundings and look for signs that she might have been followed. She quickly ate some fruit for breakfast and grabbed her jacket before going outside.

In many ways, the landscape reminded her of the state she'd recently left. Maine was beautiful, especially along the coast. It lacked the majesty of the great Rocky Mountains, but the island views and coastal sunrises held an unequaled splendor of their own.

The pines surrounding her new rental were tall and thick, softening the distant sound of the river that constantly communicated its presence as it rushed past huge boulders that had rolled down from the cliffs eons ago. The grandeur and magnificence made her feel small and insignificant.

She was drawn down the small path toward the river. The sun dappled the natural trail that was kept clean by traveling deer, elk and coyotes. Giant boulders edged the river, but the trail led around their impediment to a gentle cove of water, created when one large rock blocked a tiny portion of the river that flowed into the cove. The water eventually escaped back into the raging river, but not before it created a tiny paradise for fishing or even swimming.

The area was completely isolated, and only the birds sang in the trees as the breeze gently blew through their swaying tops. Anna could see the small rental house, up the hill behind her. She sat for a long time, perched on a rock near the cozy inlet. If the temperature was warmer she would probably go for a swim, but the chill in the air promised more cold heading this way.

She pulled the jacket close around her and walked back to the house. Without a road nearby, or any neighbors, she was truly alone and protected. For the first time in days, she began to relax.

After returning, she revived the fire and prepared some lunch. While she ate, she looked again at the book. It was very old with rare and uncommon markings inside. She had discovered a lone sheet of paper that had been folded and placed between the pages. Obviously, it had been there for a long time and had become attached to the book like a regular page.

The note said, “Meet me at midnight by the silver moon rock.” It was signed, “*Abbigail.*” The name Abbigail was also inscribed on the front page of the book. She wondered who the mysterious Abbigail was and what she had to do with her great Aunt Em. The page was old and yellowed, and seemed much older than even her aunt had been. Maybe it was a previous relative. Whoever it was, their property was now her responsibility.

Anna had lost her parents at an early age, and her aunt had taken her in, even though Aunt Em was elderly. They were the last in a long lineage and it was up to Anna to continue the bloodline.

Whatever was left by her aunt belonged to her, as she was the beneficiary of the small, impoverished estate. The book seemed to be the only item of any value, besides a few pieces of odd furniture and the album of pictures left for Anna.

When she'd shown the book to her boss, Norman, he'd chided her on carrying around such a precious work of art in an old bag. He said it was priceless and questioned her sanity. After that, the peculiar thing happened.

She was the last to leave her office that evening and decided to store the book in her desk overnight, knowing the antique store to be more secure than her apartment. On her way home, she stopped at the library and picked up an in-depth book on the subject of valuing old volumes to help in her assessment of its worth.

When she returned to her apartment, she surprised an intruder, who was lurking inside.

The room was in shambles, as if he'd been searching for something. His face was obscured when he grabbed her and put his hand across her mouth, demanding that she give him the book. Without permission, he jerked away the bag containing the library book that she held in her arms before he sent her flying across the floor as he ran out.

After calling the police and filing a complaint about the robbery, she was left alone. The experience had shaken her to her core. She phoned her roommate, who was still at her mother's house. "Kim, it was terrifying!" She explained what had happened.

Kim replied, “I’m not coming back to our apartment unless its daylight and someone is with me. You aren’t going to stay there, are you? You said they wanted a book?”

“Yes, a book my aunt left to me. It must be valuable.”

“Did anyone know you had it?”

Anna shook her head, “I don’t know. The only person I showed it to was Norman.”

With irony Kim replied, “I’d put my money on him.”

After the conversation, Anna laid her phone down. She couldn’t stay here any longer. With her hands still shaking, she began to gather items together in a suitcase because she knew the intruder would be back. She could still feel his hot breath against her cheek when he held his hand across her mouth. She shivered.

Coming to a sudden decision, she phoned Norman and demanded, “Did you tell anyone about the book?”

He reluctantly answered, “Well, yes, I did make some inquiries; it seems there is someone else who claims ownership. He wants the book back.”

Anna was speechless and could hardly answer – her anger at him was so great. “It’s mine and no one else is entitled to it! My aunt gave it to me! It was part of her estate and belongs to me.”

“Are you sure it was hers to give?”

Anna ignored the question. “Did you tell him where it was?”

“I just suggested that he get in touch with you.”

“I was mugged in my own apartment!”

Norman was nonplussed and asked, “I’m sorry, Anna. Did you lose the book?”

Tears filled her eyes at his callousness. Defensively, she blurted, “That’s none of your business!” Kim was right – or partly right. Anna still couldn’t accept that he was responsible for what happened. After a moment, she stated, “I can’t stay here and wait for someone to hurt me. If you know who did this, Norman, you need to fix it – whatever it takes.”

“Where are you going?”

“I…I don’t know!” She hung up and grabbed her suitcase. When she left, she stopped at the antique store and picked up the book. The building was dark and Norman was gone. Tomorrow, she would empty her savings account, and then disappear.

***